Grammar and Writing 6

Student Workbook

Second Edition

Christie Curtis

Mary Hake

Houghton Mifflin Harcourt Publishers, Inc.

Grammar and Writing 6

Second Edition

Student Workbook

This edition is based on the work titled *Grammar and Writing 6* © 2006 by Mary E. Hake and Christie Curtis and originally published by Hake Publishing.

Printed in the U.S.A.

ISBN 978-0-544-04427-2

6 7 8 9 10   2266   22 21 20 19 18

4500703351   B C D E F G

Contents

Introduction   1

Lesson **1**   The Sentence   2

Lesson **2**   The Paragraph, Part 1   5

Lesson **3**   The Paragraph, Part 2   9

Lesson **4**   The Paragraph, Part 3   13

Lesson **5**   The Essay: Three Main Parts   17

Lesson **6**   The Essay: Introductory Paragraph   21

Lesson **7**   The Essay: Body Paragraphs   26

Lesson **8**   The Essay: Concluding Paragraph   32

Lesson **9**   The Essay: Transitions   37

Lesson **10**   Brainstorming for Ideas   41

Lesson **11**   Writing a Complete Essay   47

Lesson **12**   Evaluating Your Essay   48

Lesson **13**   Supporting a Topic Sentence with Experiences, Examples, Facts, and Opinions   51

Lesson **14**   Supporting a Topic Sentence with Definitions, Anecdotes, Arguments, and Analogies   56

Lesson **15**   Preparing to Write a Persuasive (Argument) Essay   60

Lesson **16**   Writing the Persuasive (Argument) Essay   63

Lesson **17**   Evaluating the Persuasive (Argument) Essay   65

Lesson **18**   Writing a Strong Thesis Statement   68

Lesson **19**   Preparing to Write an Expository (Informative) Essay   70

Lesson **20**   Writing the Expository (Informative) Essay   72

Lesson **21**   Evaluating the Expository (Informative) Essay   74

Lesson **22**   Preparing to Write a Personal Narrative   77

Lesson **23**   Writing a Personal Narrative   79

Lesson **24**   Evaluating the Personal Narrative   80

Lesson **25**   Preparing to Write a Descriptive Essay   83

Lesson **26**   Writing a Descriptive Essay   87

Lesson **27**   Evaluating the Descriptive Essay   88

Lesson **28**   Writing a Chapter Summary   91

Lesson **29**   Writing a Short Story Summary   92

Lesson **30**   Developing an Outline   94

Lesson **31**   Preparing to Write a Research Paper: The Working Bibliography   97

Lesson **32**   Preparing to Write a Research Paper: Notes, Thesis, Outline   101

Lesson **33**   Writing the Research Paper   103

Lesson **34**   Evaluating the Research Paper   106

Lesson **35**   Preparing to Write an Imaginative Story   109

Lesson **36**   Writing an Imaginative Story   113

Lesson **37**   Evaluating the Imaginative Story   114

Lesson **38**   Writing in Response to Literature   117

Lesson **39**   Writing in Response to Informational Text   120

More Practice and Silly Stories

More Practice Lesson 2   122

More Practice Lesson 6   123

More Practice Lesson 9   124

Silly Story #1   125

More Practice Lesson 20   126

More Practice Lesson 26   127

Silly Story #2   128

More Practice Lesson 28   129

More Practice Lesson 31   130

More Practice Lesson 38   131

More Practice Lesson 40   133

More Practice Lesson 47   134

Silly Story #3   135

More Practice Lesson 49   137

More Practice Lesson 52   138

More Practice Lesson 56   139

More Practice Lesson 61   140

More Practice Lesson 63   141

More Practice Lesson 65   142

More Practice Lesson 69   143

More Practice Lesson 70   144

Silly Story #4   146

More Practice Lesson 73   147

More Practice Lesson 74   148

More Practice Lesson 75   150

More Practice Lesson 76   152

More Practice Lesson 90   154

More Practice Lesson 92   155

Silly Story #5   156

More Practice Lesson 98   158

Introduction

Just as a girl who wants to become a better basketball player shoots free throws every day, and just as a boy who wants to become a better guitar player plays his guitar every day, so a person who wants to become a better writer should write every day.

Further, just as the basketball player enjoys shooting the ball and the guitar player has fun trying new chords, so we should enjoy writing without worrying that what we write is going to be graded or looked at by someone else. We should write for the fun and satisfaction that it brings to us, and because practicing and trying new skills will help us to become better writers, just as practicing specific skills helps the basketball player and guitar player to become better at those activities.

A great way to practice your writing every day is to write in a journal, which can be a notebook with blank paper. When you write in a journal, you should not worry about who will read or "grade" your writing. This is a time for you simply to put your thoughts down on paper.

Of course, you do not want your writing to be so poor that it cannot be understood. It is always a good idea to practice the simple rules of grammar that you already know, such as capitalizing the first letter in a sentence or placing a period at the end of a sentence. However, it is unnecessary for you to write cautiously out of fear about your grade or about what people will think of your words. Writing in your journal is your time to shoot layups or practice scales. You may even experiment with trick shots or new chords. You will be given a suggested topic for journal writing before you start your Grammar Lesson each day.

Writing Notebook

Find a small (one-inch) three-ring binder for storing these daily journals along with your Writing Lessons. Make a divider to separate the daily journals from the Writing Lessons. Create a third section for storing ideas, memories, dreams, favorite words, or catchy phrases that you might want to use someday in an essay, story, or poem. **Plan to keep this Writing Notebook well organized.**

LESSON
1

The Sentence

The Sentence

We have learned that a **sentence** expresses a complete thought. Good sentences are the building blocks of effective writing. A good sentence can be long or short. A long sentence is not necessarily better than a short one.

Our writing goal is not to fill up a page with many words. Instead, our goal is to write clearly so that a reader says, "Aha, I see. I understand what you wrote." Too many words can confuse or bore a reader. A skillful writer makes every word count.

In this lesson, we shall practice writing sentences in which every word adds important information without being repetitive. We can do this two different ways: (1) by combining two or more sentences into one compact sentence or (2) by writing a wordy sentence another way.

Combining Sentences

Sometimes combining the information from two or more sentences can reduce the number of unnecessary words in our writing. Consider the sentences below.

WORDY: Kate wore a long coat. Kate wore heavy boots.
BETTER: Kate wore a long coat and heavy boots.

WORDY: Kate is my classmate. Kate raises chickens.
BETTER: My classmate Kate raises chickens.

WORDY: Kate laughed. Ted laughed. I did too.
BETTER: Kate, Ted, and I laughed.

WORDY: I saw cows. I saw horses. I also saw sheep.
BETTER: I saw cows, horses, and sheep.

Example 1   Combine information from the two sentences below to make one sentence.

Kate plays volleyball. Kate also plays soccer.

Instead of repeating "Kate plays," we put all the information into one compact sentence:

Kate plays volleyball and soccer.

Example 2 Combine information from the two sentences below to make one sentence.

That horse is gentle. That horse trots gracefully.

Instead of repeating "That horse," we put all the information into one compact sentence:

That gentle horse trots gracefully.

Writing It Another Way Sometimes there is a shorter, more direct way to write a sentence. Consider the following sentence:

The fence was painted by Kurt.

In the sentence above, Kurt does the action. He paints the fence. Yet, Kurt is not the subject of the sentence. We find him at the end of the sentence. Instead, "fence" is the subject, but "fence" does not act. It is only acted upon; it is painted by someone. We call this passive voice.

Whenever possible, it is better to write a sentence in which the subject does the acting (active voice), as in the sentence below:

Kurt painted the fence.

Compare the sentence pairs below.

WORDY: An apple was eaten by the gentle horse.
BETTER: The gentle horse ate an apple.

WORDY: The mouse had been frightened by a cat.
BETTER: A cat had frightened the mouse.

WORDY: They were tutored in math by Ms. Rivas.
BETTER: Ms. Rivas tutored them in math.

WORDY: He was amazed at the magnificent sunrise.
BETTER: The magnificent sunrise amazed him.

Example 3 Rewrite the sentence below in a shorter, more direct way. Use the active voice.

The car's windshield was cracked by a golf ball.

If we turn the sentence around, putting the last part first, we can make a more compact sentence in which the subject does the acting:

A golf ball cracked the car's windshield.

Example 4 Rewrite the sentence below in a shorter, more direct way. Use the active voice.

She has been comforted by her friends.

If we turn the sentence around, putting the last part first, we can make a more compact and direct sentence:

Her friends have comforted her.

Practice For 1–3, combine sentences to make one compact sentence.

1. Daisy is my cousin. Daisy cares for many animals.

   Daisy My cousin cares for Animals.

2. She feeds chickens. She feeds horses. She feeds pigs.

   she Feeds chickens, horses, & Pigs.

3. That pig is little. That pig escaped from the pen.

   The little pig escaped the pen.

For 4–6, rewrite the sentence in a shorter, more direct way. Use the active voice. (Hint: Put the last part of the sentence first.)

4. They were surprised by the news.

   _____

5. Lulu had been confused by the assignment.

   _____

6. That picture was painted by Rembrandt.

   _____

The Paragraph, Part 1

The Paragraph A **paragraph** is a group of sentences that build on a main idea, or topic. A good paragraph presents one main idea and develops it with additional sentences giving more specific information about that main idea.

The Topic Sentence The **topic sentence** is a complete sentence telling the main idea of a paragraph. Often the topic sentence is the first sentence of a paragraph, but not always. Topic sentences are underlined in the paragraphs below:

Jenny's favorite sport is softball. She takes her glove everywhere she goes so that she is always ready to play. Last Saturday she played four games of softball at the park. She hopes to do that again this Saturday. She says she would like to be a softball coach when she grows up.

————————————

This morning, Kurt tied his little sister's shoes and fixed her a bowl of cereal. At naptime, he will read her a story. Later, he will push her on the swing and play games with her in the yard. Kurt helps his little sister whenever he can.

Example 1 Underline the topic sentence in the following paragraph:

My well-to-do neighbor wears one short black sock and one long red sock underneath his sandals. Uneven suspenders hold up his baggy pants; several buttons have fallen off his shirt. He carefully plants weed seeds in the flower bed and cuts his grass with a pair of rusty scissors. My neighbor behaves like an odd character.

The paragraph above is all about things that make a certain neighbor appear odd. Therefore, we underline the topic sentence as follows:

My well-to-do neighbor wears one short black sock and one long red sock underneath his sandals. Uneven suspenders hold up his baggy pants; several buttons have fallen off his shirt. He carefully plants weed seeds in the flower bed and cuts his grass with a pair of rusty scissors. **My neighbor behaves like an odd character.**

Example 2 The paragraph below contains a sentence that does not support the topic sentence. Read the paragraph carefully. Then draw a line through the sentence that does not belong.

> Bedbugs have become a nuisance in Mrs. Smith's home. Several bedbugs hitched a ride on Mrs. Smith's coat when she flew home from abroad, and now they have multiplied. Large numbers of them live in her carpet and blankets. Mrs. Smith has an antique dresser with fancy glass knobs. Now she must wash everything to get rid of the pests.

We see that the paragraph above is all about Mrs. Smith's trouble with bedbugs. That Mrs. Smith owns an antique dresser has nothing to do with the bedbug topic, so we eliminate the sentence as follows:

> Bedbugs have become a nuisance in Mrs. Smith's home. Several bedbugs hitched a ride on Mrs. Smith's coat when she flew home from abroad, and now they have multiplied. Large numbers of them live in her carpet and blankets. ~~Mrs. Smith has an antique dresser with fancy glass knobs.~~ Now she must wash everything to get rid of the pests.

Practice and Review For paragraphs a–c, underline the topic sentence.

a.   Tucker wrote a verse inside the birthday card that he made for his mother. He also made up a poem called "The Trail of a Snail" and entered it in a contest. He is always looking for new ideas for poetry. Tucker is a poet!

b.   The discoveries of several scientists over many years resulted in the telephones we use today. In 1831, Michael Faraday proved that vibrations of metal could be converted to electrical impulses. In 1861, Johann Philip Reis created an instrument that changed sound to electricity and back again to sound. Through the years, other people continued to add to the science of sound. Finally, in 1876, Alexander Graham Bell made the first successful phone call using his own invention.

c. To increase his endurance, Jeremy rides his bicycle two miles to his friend's house and then runs three miles around the park before riding his bike home again. <u>Jeremy wants a strong, healthy body in order to become a firefighter someday.</u> He does push-ups and sit-ups daily to strengthen his muscles. He eats nutritious meals and gets plenty of sleep.

For paragraphs d–f, draw a line through the sentence that does not belong.

d. Mom said that I would forget my head if it were not attached. Last night, I left the bath water running until it spilled over onto the floor and ran down the hallway. ~~My cat's name is Whiskers.~~ I could not find my shoes this morning, so I am wearing my rain boots instead. Also, I cannot remember where I put my grammar book. Did I leave it at the library? Maybe Mom was right about my head.

e. The cuckoo family includes many interesting species of birds. Some live in trees, but others, such as roadrunners, live on the ground. Some cuckoos build no nests of their own but leave their eggs in the nests of other birds, which care for the young that hatch. Some cuckoos are insectivorous, and others eat snakes, lizards, and small rodents. Most cuckoos are brown or gray with long tails, but some are a glossy emerald green. ~~Spiders have eight legs.~~

f. The Venus flytrap is a carnivorous plant. It attracts, captures, kills, and digests insects, spiders, and slugs. People around the world have been fascinated by this peculiar plant. ~~Herons have long, pointed bills.~~ In the wild, Venus flytraps grow only in a small area along the coasts of North and South Carolina, in bogs and wetlands. Taking flytraps from their wild habitat is against the law. However, you can buy a Venus flytrap from a nursery.

For g and h, combine sentences to make one compact sentence.

g. That tree is tall. That tree has lost its leaves.

That tall tree lost its leaves.

h. We can identify trees. We can identify shrubs too.

We can identify trees, and shrubs.

For i and j, rewrite the sentence in a shorter, more direct way. Use the active voice. (Hint: Put the last part of the sentence first.)

i. A good time was had by everyone.

Everyone had a good time.

j. Molly's artwork is appreciated by many people.

Many people lik molly's artwork

_B+_

Logical Order   We have learned that a paragraph is a group of sentences that build on a main idea or topic. A good paragraph presents one main idea and develops it with additional sentences, giving more specific information about that main idea. The supporting sentences are arranged in a **logical order.** The paragraph below tells what happened first, next, and last.

> A jazz concert in the park inspired Elle to learn how to play the saxophone. First, she borrowed her grandfather's old saxophone and asked him to teach her some simple songs. He taught her everything he knew about the instrument. Next, Elle joined a jazz band at her school. She practiced with them twice a week for two years. Now, Elle is an accomplished musician.

Sometimes creating a logical order means placing sentences in order of importance, usually ending with the most important point, as in the paragraph below.

> Conrad's woodworking skills have proved beneficial in many ways. Conrad has saved money by building his own desk, tables, picture frames, and bookcases. Moreover, he now has furniture and wood pieces in precisely the size, style, and finish that he likes best. Most importantly, woodworking allows Conrad to use his creativity, which gives him pride and satisfaction.

Example   Arrange the sentences below in a logical order to create a good paragraph.

- Since no one knew a "Michael," Freddy finally took the jacket to the lost-and-found in the principal's office.

- Then, he began asking boys on the playground if they knew a "Michael."

- Freddy found a boy's jacket on the playground.

- First, he looked inside the collar, where he found the name *Michael* written in black ink.

What happened first? Then what happened? We can number the sentences like this:

4 Since no one knew a "Michael," Freddy finally took the jacket to the lost-and-found in the principal's office.

3 Then, he began asking boys on the playground if they knew a "Michael."

1 Freddy found a boy's jacket on the playground.

2 First, he looked inside the collar, where he found the name *Michael* written in black ink.

Now, we can arrange these sentences in order to make the following paragraph:

> Freddy found a boy's jacket on the playground. First, he looked inside the collar, where he found the name *Michael* written in black ink. Then, he began asking boys on the playground if they knew a "Michael." Since no one knew a "Michael," Freddy finally took the jacket to the lost-and-found in the principal's office.

Practice and Review

a. Read the sentences below. Then number them according to what happens first, next, etc. (Place numbers one through four in the boxes.)

☐ Next, she makes sure the bulb is not broken.

☐ Finally, Jenna decides that she must buy new batteries for her flashlight.

☐ On a dark night, Jen discovers that her flashlight does not work.

☐ First, she checks to see if its batteries are positioned correctly.

b. Finish writing the following paragraph, adding three or more sentences in a logical order.

I am going to plan a birthday party for my friend.

First, _____

_____

_____

_____

_____

_____

_____

_____

_____

_____

_____

c. Underline the topic sentence in the paragraph below.

Traveling across the United States by train gives me an opportunity to see the countryside: the great expanses of desert, farmland, and mountains. The train's comfortable seats, friendly conductors, and classy dining car all contribute to an enjoyable ride. On the train, I can relax, read, or chat with other passengers. I appreciate the many advantages of train travel.

d. Draw a line through the sentence that does not belong in the paragraph below.

Uncle Will has many interests. As a philatelist, he collects postage stamps. He restores antique cars, makes stained glass windows, and plays the trumpet in a band. His best friend repairs computers. Most of all, Uncle Will enjoys scuba diving off the coasts of various islands.

For e and f, combine the two sentences to make one compact sentence.

e. Linda has pretty eyes. Linda's eyes are brown.

_____

f. Snakes slither and slide. Snakes hide under rocks.

Snakes slither & slide under rocks.

For g and h, rewrite the sentence in a shorter, more direct way. Use the active voice. (Hint: Put the last part of the sentence first.)

g. Maddy's singing is liked by most people.

Most people like Maddy's singing.

h. The old house can be toured by the public.

The public can tour the old house.

LESSON 4

The Paragraph, Part 3

We have learned that a paragraph is a group of sentences building on a main idea or topic. A good paragraph presents one main idea and develops it with additional sentences giving more information about that main idea. In this lesson, we shall learn one way to produce sentences that support a topic sentence.

Supporting Sentences

You can write sentences that support a topic sentence by asking yourself these questions: *Who? What? When? Where? Why? How?* Suppose you wanted to write a paragraph using the topic sentence below.

> Walking is good exercise.

You can ask yourself the following questions:

> *Who* needs exercise?
>
> *What* makes walking good exercise?
>
> *When* can you walk?
>
> *Where* can you walk?
>
> *Why* should you walk?
>
> *How* fast or how far must you walk?

Answering the questions above will help you to create supporting sentences for your topic sentence. You might write a paragraph like this:

> Walking is good exercise. People of all ages can benefit from walking thirty minutes a day. Walking relieves stress, tones muscles, increases circulation, and strengthens the heart and lungs. People can walk at any time of the day around the block, inside a mall, through a park—anywhere. A fast walk can be energizing, a slow walk relaxing.

Example Consider this topic sentence:

> We can improve our writing.

Write some *who, what, when, where, why,* and *how* questions to get ideas for supporting sentences. Then, write a paragraph.

We can ask the following questions:

Who can improve their writing?

What can we do to improve our writing?

When can we improve our writing?

Where can we go to improve our writing?

Why do our writing skills need improving?

How can we improve our writing?

Answering the questions above helps us to write the following paragraph:

Students, teachers, young people, and older people can improve their writing. Many professional authors, novelists, poets, editors, and journalists are already excellent writers, but they can still improve. Everyone can improve. Writing every day will increase one's vocabulary, clarity, and effectiveness. Good writing is essential for our communication with others, for filling out college or job applications, and for success in any career.

Practice and Review

a. Read the sentences below. Then number them according to what happens first, next, etc. (Place numbers one through five in the boxes.)

[3] Next, he saws boards to the right lengths.

[5] Finally, Rover has a house that keeps him warm and dry.

[1] Cory has some free time, so he decides to build a house for his dog, Rover.

[4] After sawing, he nails the boards together.

[2] First, he gathers his tools, some wood, and a box of nails.

b. On the following lines, complete *who, what, when, where, why,* and *how* questions for this topic sentence: There are many things I like about my school.

Who _Abuda_____?

What _Math and history_____?

When _During school_____?

Where At school _____ ?

Why They are very Fun _____ ?

How additon and World history _____ ?

Now, in your mind, answer the questions above and on the previous page to help you finish writing the paragraph below.

There are many things I like about my school. Math and history specificaly. They are very Fun cause of additionand history OF the world, at school.

_____

_____

_____

_____

_____

_____

_____

_____

c. Underline the topic sentence in the paragraph below.

Bradley designs robotic toys. Three years ago, he discovered that he could convert his old stuffed animals into walking-and-talking robots. Using his knowledge of mechanics and technology, Bradley created a monkey that could climb a ladder, a remote-controlled alligator that could crawl across the floor and snap its jaws open and shut, and a fuzzy bear cub that could hug and say, "I love you." Bradley's next challenge is to make a motion-activated, life-sized dog to keep uninvited guests out of his garage.

d. Draw a line through the sentence that does not belong in the paragraph on the next page.

Trina organized her bookshelf. She placed all her mystery novels on the top shelf. On the middle shelf, she lined up her nonfiction books, including her dictionary and world atlas. ~~Trina has two intelligent sisters, who are like walking encyclopedias.~~ On the bottom shelf, she put her favorite books of poetry and humorous short stories.

For e and f, combine sentences to make one compact sentence.

e. Rita wore an elegant vest. It was made of satin.

Rita wore an elegant satin vest.

f. I rode my bicycle to the market. I rode my bicycle to the post office. I rode my bicycle to the library.

I rode my bicycle the market, Post office and lidrary.

For g and h, rewrite the sentence in a shorter, more direct way. Use active voice. (Hint: Put the last part of the sentence first.)

g. He was confused by my statement.

My statement confused him.

h. Daisy's older sister must have been startled by the goose.

A goose startled Daisy older sister.

Additional Practice Write a paragraph using one of the following sentences as your topic sentence or make up your own topic sentence. Add at least three sentences to support or more fully explain your topic sentence. (Think: Who? What? When? Where? Why? How?)

1. Being a good student requires self discipline.

2. There are many things I can do to help my friends.

3. Sometimes life is hard.

4. I appreciate my family.

LESSON 5

The Essay: Three Main Parts

We have learned that a paragraph is a group of sentences that build on a main idea or topic.

The Essay   An **essay** is a group of paragraphs that build on one main idea or ideas. In this lesson, we shall learn about the structure of an essay.

An essay has three main parts:

    1. Introductory Paragraph

    2. Body or Support Paragraphs

    3. Concluding Paragraph

Below is a chart that shows the structure of the typical five-paragraph essay. Each box represents one paragraph.

> Introductory Paragraph

> Body Paragraph

> Body Paragraph

> Body Paragraph

> Concluding Paragraph

Example   From memory, reproduce the chart showing the structure of a typical five-paragraph essay.

We can reproduce the chart like this:

Introductory Paragraph

Body Paragraph

Body Paragraph

Body Paragraph

Concluding Paragraph

Practice and Review   a. Read the sentences below. Then number them according to what happens first, next, etc. (Place numbers one through four in the boxes.)

[1] Doris's homework assignment is to write a humorous essay.

[4] Finally, she will begin writing the rough draft of her essay.

[3] Then, she will brainstorm for ideas to make the essay funny.

[2] She must first choose a humorous topic.

b. In your mind, answer some *who, what, when, where, why,* and *how* questions about this topic sentence: *Someday I would like to learn a new language.* Then write three or more supporting sentences to complete the paragraph.

Someday I would like to learn a new language.

I would love to learn Italian.
The reason why is so that I can
communicate with my Father in a
new language.

c. Underline the topic sentence in the paragraph below.

David has been composing music since he was twelve years old. He has written folk songs, love songs, and songs that make people laugh. David is an enthusiastic musician. He plays the tuba, the guitar, and the accordion. Next, he wants to learn to play the French horn.

d. Draw a line through the sentence that does not belong in the paragraph below.

Lillian collects worms, insects, and spiders. In her room she displays live tarantulas, an ant colony, and some silk worms that are hungrily devouring fresh mulberry leaves. Her friend Tracy is allergic to bee stings. Lillian has boxes and boxes of bugs that she has found in her house and yard: cinch bugs, crickets, cockroaches, and many more.

For e and f, combine the two sentences to make one compact sentence.

e. Quan was slicing a red apple. It was shiny.

Quan was slicing a shiny red apple.

f. My cousins fish at Big Bear Lake. They fish at the Kern River. They fish at the local reservoir.

My cousins Fish atBig Bear lake atthe kern river.

For g and h, rewrite the sentence in a shorter, more direct way. Use active voice. (Hint: Put the last part of the sentence first.)

g. The voters' poor turnout was commented on by the governor.

The govoners commented the voters poor turnout.

h. That sonata by Haydn was performed by our local orchestra.

Our local orchestra prformed sonata by Haydn

i. From memory, reproduce the chart showing the structure of a typical five-paragraph essay.

Introductory

Body

Body

Body

concluding

LESSON 6

The Essay: Introductory Paragraph

We have learned that an essay has three main parts: (1) the introductory paragraph, (2) the body paragraphs, and (3) the concluding paragraph. In this lesson, we shall learn what the introductory paragraph includes.

Introductory Paragraph

The **introductory paragraph**, the first paragraph of an essay, introduces the main subject of the essay. It tells what the entire essay is about. The introductory paragraph has two parts.

1. An introductory sentence grabs the reader's interest.

2. A thesis statement tells what the essay is about.

We can now add more detail to our chart showing the structure of an essay.

```
┌─────────────────────────────────┐
│ Introductory Paragraph          │
│    1. Introductory sentence     │
│    2. Thesis statement          │
└─────────────────────────────────┘

┌─────────────────────────────────┐
│ Body Paragraph                  │
│                                 │
│                                 │
└─────────────────────────────────┘

┌─────────────────────────────────┐
│ Body Paragraph                  │
│                                 │
│                                 │
└─────────────────────────────────┘

┌─────────────────────────────────┐
│ Body Paragraph                  │
│                                 │
│                                 │
└─────────────────────────────────┘

┌─────────────────────────────────┐
│ Concluding Paragraph            │
│                                 │
│                                 │
└─────────────────────────────────┘
```

The thesis statement is underlined in the introductory paragraph below.

There are many peculiar animals in Central America, but one of the most unusual is the two-toed sloth. <u>Three interesting characteristics set the two-toed sloth apart from most other animals</u>.

In the introductory paragraph above, the first, or introductory sentence (sometimes called the "hook") grabs the reader's attention so that he or she will keep reading. The second sentence, the thesis statement, clearly tells the reader exactly what the essay is about: three characteristics that set the two-toed sloth apart from most other animals.

The reader expects to read about these three characteristics in the body of the essay. Perhaps each of the three body paragraphs will present one interesting characteristic of the two-toed sloth.

Example 1   Underline the thesis statement in the following introductory paragraph.

While on vacation, many people camp in the mountains, but I prefer camping at the beach. The beach is the best place to camp, for there I can surf, build sand castles, and watch the seagulls.

We see that this essay gives reasons why the author prefers camping at the beach. So, we underline the second sentence.

While on vacation, many people camp in the mountains, but I prefer camping at the beach. <u>The beach is the best place to camp, for there I can surf, build sand castles, and watch the seagulls.</u>

Example 2   Complete the chart showing the structure of an essay. Include what you have learned from this lesson about the introductory paragraph.

We reproduce the chart showing the two parts of the introductory paragraph, (1) the introductory sentence and (2) the thesis statement.

```
┌─────────────────────────────────┐
│ Introductory Paragraph          │
│    1. Introductory sentence     │
│    2. Thesis statement          │
└─────────────────────────────────┘

┌─────────────────────────────────┐
│ Body Paragraph                  │
│                                 │
│                                 │
└─────────────────────────────────┘

┌─────────────────────────────────┐
│ Body Paragraph                  │
│                                 │
│                                 │
└─────────────────────────────────┘

┌─────────────────────────────────┐
│ Body Paragraph                  │
│                                 │
│                                 │
└─────────────────────────────────┘

┌─────────────────────────────────┐
│ Concluding Paragraph            │
│                                 │
│                                 │
└─────────────────────────────────┘
```

Practice and Review   a. Underline the thesis statement in the introductory paragraph below.

A close encounter with a Jerusalem cricket nearly gave Fern a heart attack last night. Insects can multiply and cause big trouble in people's homes. <u>Three of the most annoying house pests are the termite, the flea, and the ant.</u>

b. Read the sentences below. Then number them in order of importance (ending with the most important) by placing numbers two through four in the boxes.

[1] Dad rides a stationary bicycle at the gym.

[3] More importantly, he enjoys making friends with other cyclists.

[4] Most important of all, he knows that cycling keeps him physically fit.

[2] For one thing, he likes the activity—the fast pedaling, deep breathing, and logging miles.

(help.→) **c.** In your mind, think of *who, what, when, where, why,* and *how* questions for this topic sentence: We can help to conserve our natural resources. Use the answers to your questions to help you write supporting sentences to complete the paragraph.

We can help to conserve our natural resources.

_____

_____

_____

_____

_____

_____

_____

_____

_____

d. Underline the topic sentence in the paragraph below.

My friends and I plan to beautify our school. First, we shall sweep the classroom floor and clean the desks. Next, we shall rake leaves and pick up trash on the playground. In front of the school office, we shall plant a rose garden. With our parents' help, we shall plant six shade trees as well.

e. Draw a line through the sentence that does not belong in the paragraph below.

Mrs. Dalia has many flowering plants around her home. Red geraniums line the walkway to her front door. In the front yard, a lilac bush blooms amid sweet-smelling alyssum and beds of colorful snapdragons and pansies. Mrs. Dalia volunteers at the hospital. Vines of bright purple morning glories and vibrant yellow trumpets climb the brick walls of her house. The dazzling beauty takes one's breath away.

For f and g, combine sentences to make one compact sentence.

f. A jellyfish has long tentacles. They are poisonous.

Jelly Fish have poisonus tentacles.

g. Nick is my cousin. Nick plays the guitar and the bass.

My cousin, Nick, plays the bass and guitar.

h. Rewrite the sentence below in a shorter, more direct way. (Hint: Put the last part of the sentence first.)

That portrait was painted by Uncle James.

Uncle James painted that portrait.

i. From memory, complete the chart showing the structure of a typical five-paragraph essay.

Introductry **Paragraph**
1. _Introductry sentence_
2. _Thesis statement_

Body **Paragraph**

Body **Paragraph**

Body **Paragraph**

concluding **Paragraph**

The Essay: Body Paragraphs

We have learned that the introductory paragraph, the first paragraph of an essay, grabs the reader's interest and tells what the entire essay is about. In this lesson, we shall learn about the body paragraphs of an essay.

Body Paragraphs The **body paragraphs,** or support paragraphs, come after the introductory paragraph and before the concluding paragraph. Body paragraphs prove or explain the thesis statement. They provide examples, facts, opinions, or arguments to help the reader understand that the thesis statement is true.

Topic Sentence Each body paragraph has a **topic sentence** telling the reader exactly what the paragraph is about. The topic sentence is followed by supporting sentences.

Supporting Sentences **Supporting sentences** support, prove, or explain the topic sentence of that body paragraph. At least three supporting sentences are usually needed to make a strong paragraph.

Each body paragraph looks like this:

```
Topic Sentence

   1. Supporting sentence

   2. Supporting sentence

   3. Supporting sentence
```

Now we can add more detail to our chart showing the structure of an essay. To each Body Paragraph box, we can add the topic sentence and three or more supporting sentences.

Example 1 Reproduce the chart showing the structure of an essay. Add the information from this lesson about body paragraphs.

We reproduce the chart below, adding the topic sentence and three or more supporting sentences to each Body Paragraph.

```
┌─────────────────────────────────────────┐
│ Introductory Paragraph                    │
│      1. Introductory sentence             │
│      2. Thesis statement                  │
└─────────────────────────────────────────┘

┌─────────────────────────────────────────┐
│ Body Paragraph                            │
│    •Topic sentence                        │
│        1. Supporting sentence             │
│        2. Supporting sentence             │
│        3. Supporting sentence             │
├─────────────────────────────────────────┤
│ Body Paragraph                            │
│    •Topic sentence                        │
│        1. Supporting sentence             │
│        2. Supporting sentence             │
│        3. Supporting sentence             │
├─────────────────────────────────────────┤
│ Body Paragraph                            │
│    •Topic sentence                        │
│        1. Supporting sentence             │
│        2. Supporting sentence             │
│        3. Supporting sentence             │
└─────────────────────────────────────────┘

┌─────────────────────────────────────────┐
│ Concluding Paragraph                      │
│                                           │
│                                           │
└─────────────────────────────────────────┘
```

Example 2 Using the introductory paragraph below, write a topic sentence for each body paragraph to further develop the thesis statement of the essay.

> While on vacation, many people camp in the mountains, but I prefer camping at the beach. <u>The beach is the best place to camp, for there I can surf, build sand castles, and watch the seagulls.</u>

We can write the following three topic sentences to further explain our thesis statement.

Topic sentence #1: Surfing is my favorite sport.

Topic sentence #2: I love to build sand castles on the beach.

Topic sentence #3: The gliding and swooping seagulls spark my imagination.

Each of these topic sentences can be developed into a body paragraph by adding supporting sentences to further explain the topic sentence. For example, we might develop the first body paragraph like this:

topic sentence →   *Surfing is my favorite sport.* With the warm sun on my back and salty air in my lungs, I paddle with all my might to catch the best waves. The thrill of

supporting sentences { balancing on the board and being propelled toward shore atop a gigantic wave makes me want to ride more and more waves. I like to surf from sunup till sundown.

In the body paragraph above, supporting sentences follow the topic sentence to explain why surfing is the writer's favorite sport.

Practice and Review   a.   Write three topic sentences to support the thesis statement in the following introductory paragraph:

There are many admirable people in the world, but none are as admirable as my friend. <u>My friend deserves admiration for three important reasons</u>.

(Hint: Think about an admirable friend of yours. What makes that person admirable? Is he or she generous? Helpful? Kind? Compassionate? Courageous? Strong? Patient? Punctual? Considerate? Courteous? Clever? Diligent? Hardworking? Skillful at something? Knowledgeable? You might might also think, *Who? What? When? Where? Why?*)

Topic sentence #1: My Freind Muhammad is always helping and thinking of others.

Topic sentence #2: He also is in a hurry For helping the cummonity nearby.

Topic sentence #3: he always is reliable and a very good Freind.

b. Now, develop one of your topic sentences from "Practice and Review **a**" into a body paragraph. Add at least three supporting sentences.

_____

_____

_____

_____

_____

_____

_____

_____

_____

_____

c. Underline the thesis statement in the introductory paragraph below.

    Life is full of surprises, but this one beats all. I never expected my number of pets to multiply so quickly. <u>My cat, dog, and guinea pig all gave birth on the same day</u>.

d. Read the sentences below. Then number them in a logical order. (Place numbers one through four in the boxes.)

[2] There we hiked, explored, and photographed wildlife.

[1] Last spring, we camped in the desert.

[4] Perhaps this picture will win a prize in a photography contest.

[3] My best photo captured both a roadrunner and a tortoise.

e. Underline the topic sentence in the paragraph below.

Mammals have certain characteristics that make them different from other animals. For example, all mammals are warm blooded. They give birth to live young that look like smaller versions of themselves, and they nourish their young with milk. Although they might be born without hair, mammals grow hair at some stage of their development. In addition, most mammals have sweat glands.

f. Draw a line through the sentence that does not belong in the paragraph below.

Katy is preparing to adopt a beagle as a pet. First, she must make sure that the fencing around her yard is secure. Then, she will save her money so that she can purchase a collar, a leash, a food bowl, some dog food, and a water dish that will not tip over. ~~Katy used to have a hamster.~~ Also, she will make a soft bed in a warm, dry place where the beagle can sleep. Katy knows that caring for a dog is a big responsibility.

For g and h, combine the two sentences to make one compact sentence.

g. Clara zipped up her jacket. Her jacket was made of wool.

Clar zipped up her wool jacket.

h. Robert is my classmate. Robert is learning to cook.

Robert, my classmate, is learning to cook.

i. Rewrite the sentence below in a shorter, more direct way. Use the active voice. (Hint: Put the last part of the sentence first.)

The corn is husked by Phil and Jenny.

Jenny and phil husked the corn.

j. From memory, complete the chart showing the structure of a typical five-paragraph essay.

```
+-----------------------------------------------+
|  __Itroductry__ Paragraph                     |
|     1. _____                  |
|     2. __thesis statement__                   |
+-----------------------------------------------+

+-----------------------------------------------+
|  __Body__ Paragraph                           |
|     __Topic__ sentence                        |
|     1. __supporting__ sentence                |
|     2. __supporting__ sentence                |
|     3. __supporting__ sentence                |
+-----------------------------------------------+

+-----------------------------------------------+
|  __Body__ Paragraph                           |
|     __Topic__ sentence                        |
|     1. __supporting__ sentence                |
|     2. __supporting__ sentence                |
|     3. __supporting__ sentence                |
+-----------------------------------------------+

+-----------------------------------------------+
|  __Body__ Paragraph                           |
|     __Topic__ sentence                        |
|     1. __Supporting__ sentence                |
|     2. __supporting__ sentence                |
|     3. __supporting__ sentence                |
+-----------------------------------------------+

+-----------------------------------------------+
|  __Concluding__ Paragraph                     |
|                                               |
|                                               |
+-----------------------------------------------+
```

The Essay: Concluding Paragraph

We have learned about the first two main parts of an essay, the introduction and the body. In this lesson, we shall learn about the third and final main part of an essay: the conclusion.

Concluding Paragraph

The **concluding paragraph** is the final paragraph of an essay. It summarizes the ideas expressed in the body of the essay. The concluding paragraph has three important parts:

1. A restatement of the thesis statement

2. A reference to each topic sentence

3. A clincher sentence (last one)

Your "last words" will leave a lasting impression on your readers.

Notice how the concluding paragraph below refers to the three topic sentences in Example 2 of Lesson 7.

Topic sentence #1: <u>Surfing</u> is my favorite sport.

Topic sentence #2: I love to build <u>sand castles</u> on the beach.

Topic sentence #3: The gliding and swooping <u>seagulls</u> spark my imagination.

CONCLUDING PARAGRAPH:

Restatement of thesis ⟶   In conclusion, there is no better place to camp than the beach. Surfing, building sand castles, and watching seagulls are some of my favorite activities. Only at the beach can I do these things.

Reference to each topic sentence

Clincher (last sentence)

We see that the concluding paragraph above restates the thesis and contains a reference to each topic sentence. It sums up all the main ideas in the essay and ends with a strong statement. The last words will leave a lasting impression on the reader.

Example 1 Write a concluding paragraph for an essay with the following thesis statement and topic sentences:

> Thesis statement: My friend Hugo deserves admiration for three important reasons.

> Topic sentence #1: Hugo has overcome many hardships.

> Topic sentence #2: Hugo encourages others.

> Topic sentence #3: Hugo works more diligently than anyone else that I know.

Based on the thesis statement and topic sentences above, we can write a concluding paragraph like this:

> **In conclusion, most people admire my friend Hugo. He has proved himself to be an overcomer, an encourager, and a hard worker. The world would be a better place if there were more people like Hugo.**

Example 2 On the next page, complete the chart showing the structure of an essay. Include the three important parts of a concluding paragraph.

We reproduce the chart below, adding the three important parts of the concluding paragraph.

```
┌─────────────────────────────────────┐
│ Introductory Paragraph               │
│    1. Introductory sentence          │
│    2. Thesis statement               │
└─────────────────────────────────────┘

┌─────────────────────────────────────┐
│ Body Paragraph                       │
│   •Topic sentence                    │
│      1. Supporting sentence          │
│      2. Supporting sentence          │
│      3. Supporting sentence          │
└─────────────────────────────────────┘

┌─────────────────────────────────────┐
│ Body Paragraph                       │
│   •Topic sentence                    │
│      1. Supporting sentence          │
│      2. Supporting sentence          │
│      3. Supporting sentence          │
└─────────────────────────────────────┘

┌─────────────────────────────────────┐
│ Body Paragraph                       │
│   •Topic sentence                    │
│      1. Supporting sentence          │
│      2. Supporting sentence          │
│      3. Supporting sentence          │
└─────────────────────────────────────┘

┌─────────────────────────────────────┐
│ Concluding Paragraph                 │
│    1. Restatement of thesis          │
│    2. Reference to each topic        │
│       sentence                       │
│    3. Clincher sentence              │
└─────────────────────────────────────┘
```

Practice and Review a. Write a concluding paragraph based on the thesis statement "My friend deserves admiration for three important reasons" and the three topic sentences that you wrote for Lesson 7.

My Friund are the Best
you could ever wish for.

b. Underline the thesis statement in the introductory paragraph below.

The friends that we choose now can greatly affect the rest of our lives. Today we can make choices to brighten our futures. A good friend will encourage our physical fitness, our good manners, and our intellectual development.

c. Read the sentences below. Then number them according to what happens first, next, etc. (Place numbers one through four in the boxes.)

4 Daisy chases the goose away and returns to hug her cousin.

3 David stops crying, and the corners of his mouth go up as he eats the half sandwich.

1 Daisy's little cousin David is crying because a goose snatched his sandwich.

2 Then, she gives David half of her own sandwich.

d. Underline the topic sentence in the paragraph below.

Hector wrings his hands and looks at the clock. Is the minute hand moving too fast? His lips are twitching, his legs are trembling, and butterflies have invaded his stomach. He worries that words will refuse to come out of his mouth when it is time for him to speak. Hector feels very nervous about the speech that he must give in front of the class in just twenty minutes.

e. Draw a line through the sentence that does not belong in the paragraph below.

Automobile racing is now the most popular sport in the country. It received the highest rating of all sporting events on TV this year. More people attended races than any other type of sporting event last year. Carl used to ride racehorses. When people were asked what was their favorite sporting event, more said automobile racing than any other sport.

f. Combine the following two sentences to make one compact sentence: Alma repaired the engine of the yellow school bus. The school bus is gigantic.

Alma repaired the gigantic, yellow, school Bus.

g. Rewrite the sentence below using active voice. (Hint: Put the last part of the sentence first.)

Driftwood is washed to shore by the waves.

The waves washed Driftwood to shore.

h. From memory, complete the chart showing the structure of a typical five-paragraph essay.

```
┌──────────────────────────────────────────┐
│  Introductry    Paragraph                 │
│  1. Introductry sentence                  │
│  2. thesis statement                      │
└──────────────────────────────────────────┘
┌──────────────────────────────────────────┐
│    Body         Paragraph                 │
│       Topic         sentence              │
│  1. Supporting  sentence                  │
│  2. Supporting  sentence                  │
│  3. Supporting  sentence                  │
└──────────────────────────────────────────┘
┌──────────────────────────────────────────┐
│    Body         Paragraph                 │
│       Topic         sentence              │
│  1. supporting  sentence                  │
│  2. supporting  sentence                  │
│  3. supporting  sentence                  │
└──────────────────────────────────────────┘
┌──────────────────────────────────────────┐
│    Body         Paragraph                 │
│       Topic         sentence              │
│  1. supporting  sentence                  │
│  2. supporting  sentence                  │
│  3. supporting  sentence                  │
└──────────────────────────────────────────┘

┌──────────────────────────────────────────┐
│  concluding     Paragraph                 │
│  1. Restatement of  Thesis                │
│  2. Reference to each  Topic              │
│       sentence                            │
│  3. clincher sen-ence                     │
└──────────────────────────────────────────┘
```

We have learned what is contained in an essay's three main parts: the introductory paragraph, the body paragraphs, and the concluding paragraph. Although we can now write a well-organized essay, our essay will be even better if we add **transitions** to connect paragraphs.

Transitions A **transition** is a word, phrase, or clause that links one subject or idea to another. We place transitions at the beginning of paragraphs to help the essay "flow" from one paragraph to another. Transitions make the ideas easier for the reader to follow. Here are some typical transitions:

Furthermore,…	*Moreover,…*
On the other hand,…	*Aside from…*
Despite all that,…	*Instead,…*
In short,…	*Finally,…*
As a result,…	*Consequently,…*
Another thing…	*For example,…*
The second reason…	*Generally,…*
A final thing,…	*Specifically,…*
In addition,…	*Likewise,…*
In conclusion,…	

Transitions like these tell the reader

- that you are starting to support your thesis statement
- that you are going to bring up a new point
- that you are going to continue giving more information
- that you are about to conclude your essay

Transitional words and phrases can appear anywhere in a sentence.

*Mom, **too**, enjoys playing soccer.*
*Badminton is a popular sport **as well.***

Transitions will greatly improve your writing. Generally, you should have a transition at the beginning of every paragraph except for the first paragraph. Transitions linking paragraphs are underlined in the paragraphs below.

> <u>Another thing</u> I like to do is build sand castles at the beach. I fill buckets with wet sand to form walls...

> <u>In addition</u>, the swooping and gliding seagulls spark my imagination. I wonder if somehow I might be able to fly, too...

Example   Underline the transitional words in each sentence below.

(a) Furthermore, I plan to spend less time playing video games from now on.

(b) Using old buttons, Isabel decorated a lamp shade, for example.

(c) To sum up, we all became better friends as time passed.

We underline transitional words as follows:

(a) **Furthermore,** I plan to spend less time playing video games from now on.

(b) Using old buttons, Isabel decorated a lampshade, **for example.**

(c) **To sum up,** we all became better friends as time passed.

Practice and Review   Underline the transitional words in sentences a–c.

a. We shall memorize the prepositions, also. ✗

b. Besides that, I trimmed all the hedges. ✗

c. Ana, therefore, would make an outstanding distance runner.

d. Underline the thesis statement in the introductory paragraph below.

Hobbies can consume much time and money. However, I have found a hobby that is perfect for me. Collecting baseball cards is fun, inexpensive, and profitable.

e. Read the sentences below. Then number them according to what happens first, next, etc. (Place numbers one through four in the boxes.)

[2] On heavyweight beige paper, he sketches a police helicopter in flight.

[1] With pen and ink, Onping starts a new art project.

[3] Then, he adds a background of dark thunderclouds and lightning.

[4] When he finishes, Onping mats and frames his drawing.

f. Underline the topic sentence in the paragraph below.

Miss Nomer thinks no one bakes biscuits better than she. The key ingredient is mink oil, she says. She also believes that she has found the best solutions for shoe odor, dandruff, bad breath, and nail fungus. <u>Miss Nomer considers herself an expert in many areas.</u> She prides herself in giving advice about washing sweaters, styling hair, and avoiding the bird flu. Someday she will write a book, she declares.

g. Draw a line through the sentence that does not belong in the paragraph below.

The wild turkey is one of the most popular birds of North America. Benjamin Franklin wanted to have it named the national bird. These large game birds live in woods, where they eat seeds, berries, and small insects. ~~Eagles and vultures are also quite large.~~ Covered with dark feathers, wild turkeys can blend in with their wooded surroundings. People enjoy hunting wild turkeys and eating them on special occasions.

For h and i, combine the two sentences to make one compact sentence.

h. Dan wrote an essay. It was an informal, persuasive essay.

Dan wrote an informal, persuasive essay.

i. Talia has an iguana. The iguana's name is Verde.

Talia has an iguana named Verde.

j. Write the sentence below using active voice. (Hint: Put the last part of the sentence first.)

The walnuts were harvested by parrots.

The parrots harvested the walnuts.

k. From memory, complete the chart showing the structure of a typical five-paragraph essay.

Introductry Paragraph
1. _Itroductry sentence_
2. _thesis statement_

Body Paragraph
Topic sentence
1. _supporting_ sentence (8)
2. _____ sentence
3. _____ sentence

BODY Paragraph
TOPIC sentence
1. _____ sentence
2. _____ sentence
3. _____ sentence

BODY Paragraph
TOPIC sentence
1. _____ sentence
2. _____ sentence
3. _____ sentence

CONCLUDING Paragraph
1. Restatement of _THESIS_
2. Reference to each _TOPIC_ _sentence_
3. _clincher sentence_

LESSON 10

Brainstorming for Ideas

We have learned all the necessary parts of an essay, including transitions. In this lesson, we shall learn how to prepare for writing a five-paragraph essay if we are given a thesis statement.

Brainstorming **Brainstorming** is a method of quickly capturing ideas about a topic or problem. In this lesson, we shall brainstorm for ideas to create supporting paragraphs for a thesis statement. One way to brainstorm is illustrated below.

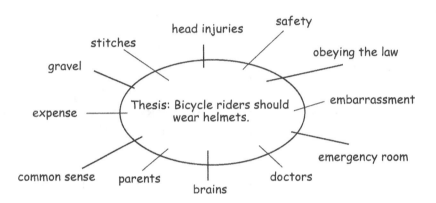

For the next few minutes, use this model to record brainstorming ideas for the thesis statement "I can do things to make the world a better place." You may use the worksheet on the following page. Quickly begin to write, in the area outside the circle, any and all words that come into your mind as soon as they enter your mind.

• Write quickly. Do not allow your pencil to stop moving.

• Do not worry about spelling or neatness.

• Do not worry about the word order or location.

• Do not think; just write.

Write for about three minutes or until your paper is covered with words, whichever comes first.

When you have finished, you will almost certainly have several ideas to help you get started writing your essay.

I can do things to make the world a better place.

help others

Be kind

Don't litter

Feed others

help

Include others

Recycle

Dentist

Police

Firefigher

Doctor

Organizing Your Ideas

After you have brainstormed, the next step is to look at the ideas that you have generated and identify the ones that best support your thesis statement. Follow these steps to organize your ideas:

1. Take a moment to look at the words or groups of words that you wrote. Some of them will relate very well to the thesis, and others will begin to look as though they do not belong or are not as strong.

2. Choose at least three different words or groups of words that best support the thesis. Circle them. If you cannot decide on just three, you may circle four or five. If you circle more than three words or groups of words, you have more than enough support for your thesis statement. You can write several body paragraphs of support, or you might later decide to combine one or more arguments or to eliminate the weaker ones.

3. These circled word groups will become your *body paragraph ideas*. Write these ideas on the lines provided below (or type them into your computer file), leaving space underneath each idea to add more notes later for expanding the paragraphs.

4. Look at your *body paragraph ideas* and try to determine the order in which they should be arranged in the body of your essay to best support your thesis. Number the ideas. You can rearrange the order or even eliminate or add additional body paragraphs at any time as ideas come to you.

1 | *Body paragraph idea:* Don't litter! Littering is bad for the Enviroment and to animals. It isn't just a good idea, but also helping the Enviroment. This will make the world a better place.

2 | *Body paragraph idea:* Help the cumunity! It is Also very helpful to help the cummunity. A Police, Fireman, Doctor and many more.

| # 3 | Body paragraph idea: There are Many. More ways to help others. Like Being kind, polite, and thank ful. You can also think of your own! |

#	Body paragraph idea: _____
	_____
	_____
	_____
	_____

Forming Topic Sentences   Once you have selected the best ideas from your brainstorming and written them on the lines, the next step is to take those ideas and form them into topic sentences. Each topic sentence will become a main idea for your essay's body paragraphs.

Practice   Write at least three topic sentences that clearly support your thesis statement. In Lesson 11, we shall expand these topic sentences into body paragraphs and then complete an essay.

Topic sentence: To not Litter and throw stuff in the garbage.

Topic sentence: helping the community.

Topic sentence: to be polite and always help others.

Topic sentence: _____

Underline the transitional words in sentences a–c.

a. Furthermore, you need to iron your wrinkled shirt. ✗

b. Lydia, on the other hand, has never been tardy. ✗

c. The old gray mare behaves similarly. ✓

d. Underline the topic sentence in the paragraph below.

A stylist at the local beauty salon cut my hair too short. She told me it looked nice, but it did not. It was shorter than my father's hair, and that is saying something because he is bald. I came home looking like a toad and wondering how I was ever going to face my friends. I shall never go back to that beauty salon again.

e. Draw a line through the sentence that does not belong in the paragraph below.

Cacti can store water in order to survive long periods of drought. During moist periods, the cactus stem swells. Then, it slowly contracts during dry periods. ~~Meteorologists predict rain for tomorrow.~~ Cacti are able to adapt to harsh conditions in which other plants would perish.

For f and g, combine the two sentences to make one compact sentence.

f. The green woodpecker has a long, sticky tongue. The tongue has a barbed point.

The green woodpecker has a long, sticky point, sticky tourge.

g. Miss Nomer wants to cut my hair. She also wants to style it.

Miss Nomer wants to cut and style my hair.

h. Rewrite the sentence below using active voice. (Hint: Put the last part of the sentence first.)

Several sonatas were played by the young pianist.

The young pianist played several sonatas

i. From memory, complete the chart showing the structure of a typical five-paragraph essay.

```
┌─────────────────────────────────────────┐
│  _____ Paragraph            │
│     1. _____            │
│     2. _____            │
└─────────────────────────────────────────┘

┌─────────────────────────────────────────┐
│  _____ Paragraph            │
│        _____ sentence           │
│     1. _____ sentence           │
│     2. _____ sentence           │
│     3. _____ sentence           │
└─────────────────────────────────────────┘

    ┌─────────────────────────────────────────┐
    │  _____ Paragraph            │
    │        _____ sentence           │
    │     1. _____ sentence           │
    │     2. _____ sentence           │
    │     3. _____ sentence           │
    └─────────────────────────────────────────┘

        ┌─────────────────────────────────────────┐
        │  _____ Paragraph            │
        │        _____ sentence           │
        │     1. _____ sentence           │
        │     2. _____ sentence           │
        │     3. _____ sentence           │
        └─────────────────────────────────────────┘

┌─────────────────────────────────────────┐
│  _____ Paragraph            │
│  1. Restatement of _____            │
│  2. Reference to each _____           │
│        _____                  │
│  3. _____                     │
└─────────────────────────────────────────┘
```

Writing a Complete Essay

In Lesson 10, you brainstormed and created ideas to support the thesis statement "I can do things to make the world a better place." You also chose the best of those ideas and put them in the order that most strongly supports the thesis statement. Then you used the ideas to create topic sentences. Now you are ready to write the complete essay.

Practice Using the topic sentences that you wrote for Lesson 10, follow the steps below to complete the essay.

1. For each topic sentence, write a body paragraph to support the thesis statement. To expand your paragraph, you might ask yourself these questions: *Who? What? When? Where? Why? How?* Your answers to these questions will give you ideas for supporting sentences.

2. Create an introductory paragraph with an introductory sentence (a "hook") that will grab the reader's interest and a sentence that states the thesis.

3. Write a concluding paragraph that includes a restatement of the thesis, a reference to each of the topic sentences, and a clincher statement.

4. Add transitions between body paragraphs to make your ideas easier for the reader to follow. Pay special attention to the transition into the concluding paragraph.

5. Finally, put all the parts together to form a complete essay. As you are working, make any necessary corrections to your previous work. You might add or subtract words or make any other change that results in a more effective essay. **Keep this essay in your three-ring binder.** You will evaluate it in the next lesson.

LESSON 12

Evaluating Your Essay

The Writing Process

All of the writing that we do should be viewed as "work in progress." Even after you have turned in an essay to your teacher for a grade, you should not feel it can never be touched again. The knowledge that *writing is a process* should guide your thinking throughout the construction of an essay. From the first steps in organizing your thoughts, to creating body paragraphs, to adding transitions, you should feel free to make changes to improve your work.

At each step of the writing process, you should stop to re-evaluate both your thoughts and the words that you have placed on the page.

It is helpful to do this after each step of the writing process. It is also important to do this after the entire essay is written. In fact, it is probably most helpful to complete an essay, then walk away from it for a day or two, and finally come back and read it again.

Many times, sentences that seemed good the first time appear much different a day or two later. Furthermore, you may find that more ideas have come to you or ideas that were somewhat muddled before have become clearer. Two days later, you can write them in a way that is more meaningful to the reader.

Use the following guidelines to help you evaluate your writing.

Evaluating Your Writing

Do not be afraid to change what you have already written. Just because it was typed or written on paper in ink does not mean it cannot be improved.

Ask yourself these questions throughout the writing process:

- Is my introductory sentence interesting? *If it is not interesting to you, it certainly will not be interesting to the reader.*

- Do I have a thesis statement that clearly explains the subject of this essay? (For this assignment, the thesis was given to you.)

- Does my thesis statement clearly state my position?

- Does each body paragraph have a clear topic sentence at the beginning that tells the reader exactly what the paragraph will be about? *Read each topic sentence without the rest of the paragraph to see if it can stand alone as a strong idea.*

- Are there other sentences that I can add to help improve my credibility and help the reader to better understand my point?

- Have I described my emotions and feelings so well that they create a picture in the mind of the reader that helps him or her feel the same as I?

- Does each paragraph (except for the first) begin with an effective transition?

- Are there other arguments that I can add as additional body paragraphs to help me prove my point?

- Are some of my arguments weak and unconvincing? Should they be removed because they do not help me prove my point?

- Do my body paragraphs appear in the best possible order to prove my point? Could I place them in a different order that is more logical or effective?

- Is each sentence constructed as well as it should be? *Read each sentence in each paragraph as if it were the only sentence on the page. This helps you to catch sentence fragments, run-on sentences, misspellings, and grammatical errors. If you are working on a computer, put blank lines between each sentence, so you only actually see one full sentence at a time on your screen. This will make sentence fragments jump out at you.*

- Does my concluding paragraph summarize and reinforce the ideas and opinions expressed in the essay? Is there a reference to each topic sentence? Is there a clincher sentence?

Practice   Use the Evaluation Form on the following page to evaluate the essay you wrote for Lesson 11. Read your essay carefully as you check for the items listed on the Evaluation Form. Write YES or NO in the blank next to each question.

When you are finished, you will either be confident that you have a strong essay, or you will know where it needs to be improved.

If you answered NO to one or more of the questions on the Evaluation Form, rewrite to improve those areas.

When you can answer YES to every question on the Evaluation Form, you will have completed this assignment.

Essay Evaluation Form

Thesis: _____

_____✓_____ Is my introductory sentence interesting? *If it is not interesting to you, it certainly will not be interesting to the reader.*

_____ Do I have a thesis statement that clearly explains the subject of this essay?

_____ Does my thesis statement clearly state my position?

_____✓_____ Does each body paragraph have a clear topic sentence at the beginning that tells the reader exactly what the paragraph will be about? *Read each topic sentence without the rest of the paragraph to see if it can stand alone as a strong idea.*

_____✓_____ Have I included sentences that improve my credibility and help the reader to better understand my point?

_____ Have I described my emotions and feelings so well that they create a picture in the mind of the reader that helps him or her feel the same as I?

_____✓_____ Does each paragraph (except for the first paragraph) begin with an effective transition?

_____✓_____ Are there no other arguments that I can add as additional body paragraphs to help me prove my point?

_____✓_____ Are all of my arguments strong and convincing? Do they all help to prove my point?

_____✓_____ Do my body paragraphs appear in the best possible order to prove my point? Is their order logical and effective?

_____✓_____ Is each sentence structured as well as it could be? *Read each sentence in each paragraph as if it were the only sentence on the page. This helps you to identify fragments, run-on sentences, and the overall strength or weakness of each sentence.*

_____✓_____ Does my concluding paragraph summarize and reinforce the ideas and opinions expressed in the essay?

LESSON 13

Supporting a Topic Sentence with Experiences, Examples, Facts, and Opinions

We remember that supporting sentences uphold, prove, or explain the topic sentence of that paragraph. We have learned to use *who, what, when, where, why*, and *how* questions that help us find sentences designed to reinforce a topic sentence. In this lesson, we shall discover additional ways to create supporting sentences.

Experiences   Your **experiences** or the experiences of other people can strongly support a topic sentence. An experience sentence explains or illustrates an event that supports the topic sentence. Consider the experience sentences below:

> In the spring, I saw wildflowers popping up among the charred remains of pine trees in the aftermath of the worst forest fire of the century. I also noticed tiny new trees sprouting—a reminder that life goes on after a tragedy, that there is always hope.

Examples   Like experiences, **examples** can describe or illustrate events that help to prove, support, or explain your topic sentence. Consider the following example sentence:

> For example, the wildflowers will attract birds and insects that will do their part to spread seeds and pollinate plants, thereby bringing new life to the forest.

Facts   A **fact** is a piece of information that can be proven to be true. You can use a fact from research to support or prove your topic sentence. Consider the fact sentence below:

> The ranger said that forest fires clean out old growth and add to the soil essential nutrients for new growth....

Experiences, examples, and facts are always the strongest arguments to prove a point, so they should immediately follow the topic sentence to build a strong paragraph.

Opinions   Your **opinions** are your thoughts or feelings about a particular subject. A fact is something that can be proven true, but an opinion is something that cannot be proven true or false. For example, it is a fact that Alaska is the largest state in the Union. It is opinion to say that Alaska is the most beautiful state in the Union.

Opinion sentences, communicating thoughts and feelings that are directly related to the topic sentence, may follow experience, example, and fact sentences to further develop the body paragraph. Consider the opinion sentences below:

Backpacking in the High Sierras during the month of January is challenging but fun.

No sport is more exciting to watch than basketball.

Playing chess and writing letters are terrific ways to spend a rainy day.

Example   Use experience, example, fact, and opinion sentences to support the following topic sentence:

We can learn much from the ant.

We can write the following sentences to support the topic sentence above:

Experience sentence: In August we had repeated ant infestations, proving that ants never admit defeat. Likewise, I shall never be defeated.

Example sentence: For example, ant colonies display how working together can bring good results.

Fact sentence: According to the encyclopedia, ants are one of the most successful groups of insects in the animal kingdom because they form such highly organized colonies in which millions of ants work together.

Opinion sentence: I think that we would all be happier if we worked without complaining the way ants do.

Practice and Review

a. Write experience, example, fact, and opinion sentences to support this topic sentence:

Good nutrition will improve your health.

Experience sentence: When we orderd Food once I got a stomach ache. But when I eat healthy I don't.

Example sentence: For Example, salad is good for you while junk is bad and won't improve health.

Fact sentence: Did you know that Eating to much sugar can cause Diabetes which is really bad health.

Opinion sentence: I think We should all stay healthy and eat home-made Food.

Underline the transitional words in sentences b–d.

b. First, she used a power sander to smooth both sides of the cabinet door.

c. Her face, hands, and clothing were covered with sawdust as a result.

d. Therefore, she plugged in the vacuum cleaner.

e. Underline the topic sentence in the paragraph.

> After hiking along the creek, Art begins scratching his ankles, which are covered with red blisters. The more he scratches, the more his ankles itch. Later, he notices that the rash is spreading over his legs, arms, and hands. He can hardly stand the burning and itching sensation. It drives him crazy.

Thrashing and squirming, he yells, "Help!" Art is having a bad reaction to poison ivy.

f. Draw a line through the sentence that does not belong in the paragraph below.

For many reasons, Jessica did not sleep well last night. Loud cat fights outside her window kept her awake until midnight. Then she could not stop thinking about her pretty friend Karen and about how unfair it is that some girls are so much prettier than others. Just as Jessica started dozing, her sister began talking loudly in her sleep about swollen tonsils, peach-flavored lip gloss, and dictation tests, which reminded Jessica that she had not studied for her history test. She worried about that test until the alarm went off at six a.m. Jessica does not like peach-flavored lip gloss.

For g and h, combine the two sentences to make one compact sentence.

g. Minh sent me an e-mail. The e-mail was short and friendly.

_____

_____

h. Maria caught two rainbow trout. She also caught three bass.

_____

_____

i. Rewrite the sentence below using active voice. Hint: Put the last part of the sentence first.

The catfish are usually fed by Emil.

_____

j. From memory, complete the chart showing the structure of a typical five-paragraph essay.

Itroductry **Paragraph**
1. _____
2. _Thesis statement_

Body **Paragraph**
_____ sentence
1. _____ sentence
2. _____ sentence
3. _____ sentence

Body **Paragraph**
_____ sentence
1. _____ sentence
2. _____ sentence
3. _____ sentence

Body **Paragraph**
_____ sentence
1. _____ sentence
2. _____ sentence
3. _____ sentence

concluding **Paragraph**
1. Restatement of _Thesis_
2. Reference to each _Topic_
   sentence
3. _____

LESSON 14

Supporting a Topic Sentence with Definitions, Anecdotes, Arguments, and Analogies

We have learned that a topic sentence states the main idea of a paragraph and that the remainder of the paragraph should clearly and completely prove that the topic sentence is true.

We have practiced developing a body paragraph with experiences, examples, facts, and opinions. In this lesson, we shall discuss other ways to support a topic by adding detailed information that relates to the topic sentence. We can support a topic sentence by adding definitions, anecdotes, arguments, and analogies. We shall use these methods of building paragraphs when we write essays in later lessons.

Below, we shall add definitions, anecdotes, arguments, and analogies to support the following topic sentence:

Teachers should smile more on test days.

Definitions To explain the topic sentence, we can define a term or a concept. **Definitions** may help the reader to understand more fully the meaning of the topic sentence.

> Teachers should smile more on test days. *A test is an examination intended to determine whether or not a student has learned the material.*

Anecdotes To entertain the reader while illustrating our point, we can write an **anecdote,** a short account of an incident. An incident can be something that happened to us or to someone we know, and should relate to the topic sentence.

> Teachers should smile more on test days. *Entering the classroom last Friday, I was so worried about my dictation test that I could not remember my name! Ms. Crabapple's scowl made me even more nervous as I struggled to write the first word.*

Arguments In some kinds of writing, especially in persuasive writing, logical **arguments** can help to support our topic sentence. An argument might seek to disprove an opposing viewpoint.

> Teachers should smile more on test days. *Some teachers think it is their job to remain stern, but I*

believe smiling can help students relax and do better work.

Analogies Sometimes we can use an **analogy** to clarify a point. An analogy is a comparison. To be effective, the two things being compared must have many similarities. Usually interesting to a reader, an analogy will help the reader to better understand the topic sentence.

Teachers should smile more on test days. *Like a warm bath or beautiful music, a smile can make people feel more comfortable.*

<u>**Practice and Review**</u> For a–f, use this topic sentence: *We need to brush and floss our teeth to prevent tooth decay and gingivitis.*

a. Write a *definition* that could be used to expand the topic sentence above.

People should Floss and brush their teeth to stay healthy! Then you won't get tooth decay or gingivitis.

b. Write an *example* that might follow the topic sentence above.

Four years ago I had a cavity removed which hurt a lot! And it was cause I didn't floss or brush.

c. Write a *fact* to support the topic sentence.

Did you know that we brush our teeth to remove plaque, a layer of Bacteria.

d. Write an *anecdote* to illustrate the topic sentence.

_____

_____

e. Write an *argument* that might prove the topic sentence.

_____

_____

f. Write an *analogy,* or comparison, to clarify the topic sentence.

_____

_____

Underline the transitional words in sentences g and h.

g. Afterward, we (thought) about (how) we could have (done) it (better.)

h. She (accomplished her goal,) however.

i. Underline the topic sentence in the paragraph below.

Penny carefully places her books in alphabetical order on a shelf, but her twin, Jenny, just tosses hers on the floor. Jenny does not mind that her ponytail is crooked or that her socks do not match, while Penny must have every hair in place and every part of her outfit coordinated in matching colors. Likewise, Penny's clothes hang neatly in her closet, yet Jenny's lie in heaps here and there around the bedroom. <u>Although they are twins, Penny and Jenny are very different from each other.</u>

j. Draw a line through the sentence that does not belong in the paragraph below.

The giant anteater, the largest species of anteater, lives in the grasslands and rainforests of Central and South America. It can grow to a length of up to eight feet and a weight of sixty-five to one hundred forty pounds. Covered with stiff, straw-like brown or gray hair, the giant anteater has a diagonal black and white shoulder stripe. Its long, sticky tongue can rapidly extend two feet in order to trap the ants, termites, and grubs that make up its diet. ~~Sometimes people eat chocolate-covered ants.~~

k. Combine the two sentences below to make one compact sentence.

Kyle polished his boots. The boots were black and made of leather.

Kyle polished his black leather boots.

l. Rewrite the sentence below using active voice. (Hint: Put the last part of the sentence first.)

The teacher's instructions were misunderstood by half the class.

Half the class misunderstood the teacher's instruction

m. From memory, complete the chart showing the structure of a typical five-paragraph essay.

```
_____ Paragraph
    1. _____
    2. _____
```

```
_____ Paragraph
    _____ sentence
    1. _____ sentence
    2. _____ sentence
    3. _____ sentence
```

```
_____ Paragraph
    _____ sentence
    1. _____ sentence
    2. _____ sentence
    3. _____ sentence
```

```
_____ Paragraph
    _____ sentence
    1. _____ sentence
    2. _____ sentence
    3. _____ sentence
```

```
_____ Paragraph
    1. Restatement of _____
    2. Reference to each _____
       _____
    3. _____
```

Preparing to Write a Persuasive (Argument) Essay

Four Purposes for Writing

There are four basic types of writing: narrative, expository, descriptive, and persuasive. Each of these types has a different purpose.

Narrative writing tells a story or relates a series of events. A composition describing your explorations among rocks and tide pools along the ocean shore would be narrative writing. In a later lesson, you will write a narrative essay telling about a personal experience of your choice.

Expository writing gives information or explains. An article entitled "How the Internet Has Changed Our Lives" would be an example of expository writing. Another example was your essay explaining things that you can do to make the world a better place.

Descriptive writing describes a person, place, or thing. Examples include a brochure describing the giant redwoods in the Pacific Northwest, a personal composition about your best friend, and a "Lost Kitten" poster describing the appearance of the lost kitten. Later you will practice this type of writing by describing a person that you see often.

Persuasive (Argument) writing attempts to convince someone to do or believe something. An advertisement for your yard clean-up services, an article about the importance of conserving water during a drought, and a campaign flyer urging voters to elect a certain candidate are all examples of persuasive writing. In this lesson, you will write a persuasive essay.

The Persuasive (Argument) Essay

Keeping in mind the structure of a complete essay, we shall prepare to write a persuasive (argument) essay using the following sentence as our thesis statement:

Middle school students should be required to take a cooking class.

The goal of this essay will be to convince or *persuade* the reader that middle school students should be required to take a cooking class.

Persuasive essays usually deal with controversial topics, subjects that have two sides. If you prefer, you may argue the opposite side and rewrite the thesis statement to read, "Middle school students *should not* be required to take a cooking class."

As you do your brainstorming for this exercise, you will discover whether there are enough strong arguments to support your thesis. This is why brainstorming before you write is such an important exercise. It saves you a great deal of time by convincing you that your thesis statement can or cannot be supported as well as giving you the main ideas for all of your topic sentences.

Your essay will prove that your thesis statement is correct. You will use several arguments to convince the reader of this.

Brainstorming

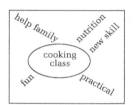

Brainstorming is always our first step in writing an essay. Recall that we draw a circle in the middle of a blank sheet of paper. Inside the circle, write the thesis statement. Then quickly begin to write in the area outside the circle any and all words that come into your mind as soon as they come into your mind.

- Write quickly and do not worry about spelling or neatness.

- Write for about three minutes or until your paper is covered with words, whichever comes first.

- As you write, continue to read your thesis statement in the middle of the circle. This will keep you focused.

Organizing Your Ideas

After you have brainstormed, look at the ideas that you have generated and identify the ones that best support your thesis statement. Follow these steps to organize your ideas:

1. Take a moment to look at the words or groups of words you wrote. Some of them will begin to stand out as relating very well to the thesis; they will firmly argue your point and convince the reader. Others will begin to look as though they do not belong or are not as strong.

2. Choose at least three different words or groups of words that best support the thesis. Circle them. If you cannot decide on just three, you may circle four or five. If you circle more than three words or groups of words, you have more than enough support for your thesis statement. You can write several body paragraphs of support, or you might

later decide to combine one or more arguments. You might even decide to eliminate the weaker ones.

3. These circled word groups will become your *body paragraph ideas*. Write these ideas on a separate piece of paper, leaving space underneath each idea to add more notes later for expanding the paragraphs.

4. Look at your body paragraph ideas and try to determine the order in which they should be arranged in the body of your essay to best support your thesis. Number the ideas. You can rearrange the order or even eliminate or add body paragraphs at any time as ideas come to you.

Forming Topic Sentences   Once you have selected the best ideas from your brainstorming and placed them on a separate page, take those ideas and form them into topic sentences. Each topic sentence will become a main idea for your essay's body paragraphs.

Practice   Write at least three topic sentences that clearly support your thesis statement. In Lesson 16, you will develop these topic sentences into body paragraphs and then complete the persuasive (argument) essay.

Topic sentence: _____

_____

_____

Topic sentence: _____

_____

_____

Topic sentence: _____

_____

_____

Topic sentence: _____

_____

_____

Writing the Persuasive (Argument) Essay

In Lesson 15, you prepared to write your persuasive (argument) essay. By brainstorming, you gathered ideas. You chose the best of those ideas and put them in the order that best supported your thesis statement. Then you used the ideas to create at least three topic sentences. Now you are ready to write the complete essay.

Practice Using the topic sentences you wrote for Lesson 15, follow the steps below to complete the persuasive (argument) essay.

1. For each topic sentence, write a body paragraph to support the thesis statement. Refer back to Lessons 13 and 14 for different ways to expand a topic sentence into a paragraph. In addition to experience and opinion sentences, you might write definitions, examples, facts, anecdotes, arguments, or analogies that support the topic sentence.

2. Create an introductory paragraph and a concluding paragraph. Remember that the introductory sentence should grab the reader's interest and that the "last words" of your conclusion will leave a lasting impression.

3. Add transitions between body paragraphs to make your ideas easier for the reader to follow. Pay special attention to the transition into the concluding paragraph.

4. Finally, put all the parts together to form a complete essay. As you are working, make any necessary corrections to your previous work. You might add things, delete things, or make any other change that results in a more convincing, persuasive essay. Keep your style formal, avoiding the use of such words as *I, me, my, we,* and *us.*

Additional Practice (Optional) After you have evaluated your persuasive (argument) essay using the guidelines in Lesson 17, you might try writing another persuasive essay on one of the following topics. Choose "should" or "should not" to complete your thesis statement.

1. Dogs and other pets (should, should not) be allowed in our national parks.

2. Our school day (should, should not) be shortened by one hour.

3. School cafeterias (should, should not) sell soda to students.

4. Bears (should, should not) be allowed to roam free in areas where people live.

5. Students (should, should not) be allowed to bring cell phones to school.

6. Our school week (should, should not) be lengthened to six days.

7. Students (should, should not) be required to do homework on weekends and holidays.

Evaluating the Persuasive (Argument) Essay

We have learned that all of the writing that we do is "work in progress." The knowledge that *writing is a process* guides our thinking throughout the construction of an essay. From the first steps in organizing our thoughts, to creating body paragraphs, to adding transitions, we constantly make changes to improve our work.

At each step of the writing process, we should stop to re-evaluate both our thoughts and the words we have placed on the page.

Evaluating Your Writing

In Lesson 16, you completed your persuasive (argument) essay. Now that some time has passed, you are ready to evaluate it using the following guidelines.

Ask yourself these questions:

- Is my introductory sentence ("hook") interesting? *If it is not interesting to you, it certainly will not be interesting to the reader.*

- Does my thesis statement clearly state my position?

- Does each body paragraph have a clear topic sentence at the beginning that tells the reader exactly what the paragraph will be about? *Read each topic sentence without the rest of the paragraph to see if it can stand alone as a strong idea.*

- Does each of my topic sentences strongly support my thesis statement?

- Are there other personal experiences, facts, examples, arguments, anecdotes, or analogies that I can add to help improve my credibility and help the reader to better understand my point?

- In my opinion sentences, have I described my emotions and feelings so well that they create a picture in the mind of the reader that helps him or her feel the same as I?

- Does each paragraph (except for the first) begin with an effective, relational transition?

- Are there other arguments that I can add as additional body paragraphs to help me prove my point?

- Are some of my arguments weak and unconvincing? Should they be removed because they do not help me prove my point?

- Do my body paragraphs appear in the best possible order to prove my point? Could I place them in a different order that is more logical or effective?

- Is each sentence constructed as well as it should be? *Read each sentence in each paragraph as if it were the only sentence on the page. This helps you to find and correct sentence fragments, run-on sentences, misspellings, and grammatical errors.*

- Does my concluding paragraph summarize and reinforce the ideas and opinions expressed in the essay? Have I convinced the reader that my thesis statement is true? Does my essay end with a powerful clincher sentence?

Practice Use the Evaluation Form on the next page to evaluate the persuasive essay that you wrote for Lesson 16. Read your essay carefully as you check for the items listed on the Evaluation Form. Write YES or NO in the blank next to each question.

When you are finished, you will either be confident that you have a strong essay, or you will know where it needs to be improved.

If you answered NO to one or more of the questions on the Evaluation Form, rewrite to improve those areas.

When you can answer YES to every question on the Evaluation Form, you will have completed this assignment.

Persuasive Essay Evaluation Form

Thesis: _____

_____ Is my introductory sentence interesting? *If it is not interesting to you, it certainly will not be interesting to the reader.*

_____ Do I have a thesis statement that clearly explains the subject of this essay?

_____ Does my thesis statement clearly state my position?

_____ Does each body paragraph have a clear topic sentence at the beginning that tells the reader exactly what the paragraph will be about? *Read each topic sentence without the rest of the paragraph to see if it can stand alone as a strong idea.*

_____ Are there no other experiences, facts, or examples that I can add to help improve my credibility and help the reader to better understand my point?

_____ In my opinion sentences, have I described my emotions and feelings so well that they create a picture in the mind of the reader that helps him or her feel the same as I?

_____ Does each paragraph (except for the first paragraph) begin with an effective transition?

_____ Are there no other arguments that I can add as additional body paragraphs to help me prove my point?

_____ Are all of my arguments strong and convincing?

_____ Do my body paragraphs appear in the best possible order to prove my point?

_____ Is each sentence structured as well as it could be? *Read each sentence in each paragraph as if it were the only sentence on the page. This helps you to identify fragments, run-on sentences, and the overall strength or weakness of each sentence.*

_____ Does my concluding paragraph summarize and reinforce the ideas and opinions expressed in the essay? Is there a clincher sentence?

LESSON 18

Writing a Strong Thesis Statement

The thesis statement clearly tells what the entire essay is about. We have practiced writing a complete essay based on an assigned thesis statement. In this lesson, we shall practice creating our own thesis statements for assigned topics.

We remember that the thesis statement not only tells the reader exactly what the essay is about but also clearly states the writer's position on the topic.

Brainstorming When faced with an assigned topic, we prepare by brainstorming in order to generate ideas and thoughts.

The first step in brainstorming is choosing your direction. You would not get into a car and just begin to drive, expecting to arrive at nowhere in particular. You need to know where you are going before you leave the driveway. In other words, you must think about the topic, choose your direction or focus, and prepare to define what your essay is about.

For example, if the assignment is to write about the qualities that make a good leader, your thesis statement could begin, "The qualities that make a good leader are …"

After brainstorming about the topic, perhaps you have decided that there are four specific qualities that make a good leader. If so, your thesis statement might be the following:

> *There are four important qualities that make a good leader.*

Practice Below and on the next page are nine topics that could be given to you as subjects for essays. For each topic, brainstorm briefly. Then write a declarative sentence that could be used as a strong thesis statement for a complete essay.

1. The things that people like most about you

_____

_____

2. The things that you would like to change about yourself if you could

_____

_____

3. What kinds of things make your family happy

_____

_____

4. Why a person should go to college

_____

_____

5. What you will do differently as a student this year from what you did last year

_____

_____

6. Ways that you can help around the house

_____

_____

7. The most interesting things to do during summer

_____

_____

8. Things that make someone seem smart

_____

_____

9. Careers that interest you

_____

_____

LESSON 19

Preparing to Write an Expository (Informative) Essay

The purpose of expository writing is to inform or explain. Expository writing tells why or how. The following might be titles for expository essays:

"New Medical Technology"

"How to Use a Thesaurus"

"Where to Find the Best Chow Mein"

"Why the Gopher Snake Makes a Good Pet"

"Building a Doghouse"

A good expository (informative) essay is well organized and clear, using precise language and definitions where necessary. It might offer an explanation of how something works, information about a specific subject, or instructions for doing something.

In this lesson, we shall prepare to write an expository essay that explains how to plan a birthday party.

Our goal is to write easy-to-follow instructions, which will require a detailed description of the process. Therefore, we shall break down the actions and carefully sequence them in a logical or practical order so that the reader can understand our step-by-step method of planning a birthday party.

Brainstorming To generate thoughts and ideas, we shall brainstorm before creating a thesis statement for our *how-to* essay.

• Write quickly and do not worry about spelling or neatness.

• Write for about three minutes or until your paper is covered with words, whichever comes first.

• Include relevant facts, concrete details, quotations, or examples.

Writing a Thesis Statement Now it is time to state the purpose of your essay in a clear thesis statement. Using the ideas you have written by brainstorming, write a sentence that tells what your essay is about.

(Hint: Will you be presenting a certain number of *steps* in your how-to essay? Or, will you be explaining a number of different *parts* of a birthday party that need to be planned? Your thesis statement will reveal your presentation plan.)

Organizing Your Ideas   After you have written a strong thesis statement telling what your essay is about, examine the ideas you have generated by brainstorming and identify the ones that best support your thesis statement. Then you might create thought clusters based on the ideas that you generated while brainstorming. You should have at least three of these clusters to create your body paragraphs.

Tone   The **tone** of an essay reflects the writer's attitude toward the topic. One's attitude, or tone, can be formal or informal, sarcastic or straightforward, serious or silly, appreciative or critical, objective or opinionated. Before you begin writing, you must decide on your tone. An expository essay is formal and objective in tone, presenting facts rather than opinions and avoiding the use of first person pronouns, such as *I, me, my, we, us,* and *our.*

Forming Topic Sentences   Once you have decided on your tone, selected the main ideas from your brainstorming, and arranged them in clusters, take those ideas and form them into topic sentences. Each topic sentence will become a main idea for your essay's body paragraphs.

Practice   Write a thesis statement and at least three topic sentences that clearly explain your thesis statement. In the next lesson, we shall develop these topic sentences into body paragraphs and then complete the expository (informative) essay.

THESIS STATEMENT: _____

_____

_____

Topic sentence: _____

_____

_____

Topic sentence: _____

_____

_____

Topic sentence: _____

_____

_____

LESSON 20

Writing the Expository (Informative) Essay

In Lesson 19, you prepared to write your expository essay about how to plan a birthday party. By brainstorming, you gathered ideas and wrote a thesis statement. You chose the best of those ideas and put them into clusters. Then you used the main ideas to create at least three topic sentences. Now you are ready to write the complete essay.

Practice Using the topic sentences that you wrote for Lesson 19, follow the steps below to complete the expository (informative) essay.

1. For each topic sentence, write a body paragraph to support the thesis statement. Refer to your notes and use your ideas to write body sentences that further explain, or expand, each topic sentence. Remember that your tone should be objective.

2. Create an introductory paragraph. Remember that the introductory sentence ("hook") should grab the reader's interest. Your thesis statement will clearly tell what the essay is about.

3. Create a concluding paragraph that refers to each topic sentence in your body paragraphs. Remember that the "last words" of your conclusion will leave a lasting impression.

4. Add transitions between body paragraphs to make your ideas easier for the reader to follow. Transitions that indicate order, such as "the first step..." or "the second step...," are appropriate in a how-to essay. Pay special attention to the transition into the concluding paragraph. Look back at Lesson 9 for help with transitions. Use appropriate links to join connected ideas within your essay.

5. Finally, put all the parts together to form a complete essay. As you are working, make any necessary corrections to your previous work. You might add things, delete things, or make any other change that results in a clearer, easier-to-follow expository essay. Maintain a formal style. Consider using multimedia, illustrations, or graphics if these will help reader understanding.

Additional Practice (Optional) After you have evaluated your expository essay using the guidelines in Lesson 21, you might try writing another expository essay on a topic of your choice or on one of these topics:

1. Explain how to play a game, any game that you know how to play.

2. Write an essay giving at least three reasons why U.S. citizens are fortunate to live in this country.

3. Give instructions for making a meal that you like.

4. Explain in detail how you would like to redecorate the room in which you are sitting, or another room in your school or home.

5. Compare and contrast the duck and the goose.

6. Tell how to construct a bookmark, a necklace, a kite, a paper airplane, or some other craft of your choice.

7. Compare and contrast a typical day in the life of a veterinarian and an elementary-school teacher.

8. Explain why you admire a particular person.

Evaluating the Expository (Informative) Essay

Remember that all of our writing is "work in progress." The knowledge that *writing is a process* guides our thinking throughout the construction of an essay. Throughout the steps of brainstorming, organizing our thoughts, creating body paragraphs, and adding transitions, we constantly make changes to improve our work.

Evaluating Your Writing

In Lesson 20, you completed your expository (informative) essay. Now that some time has passed, you are ready to evaluate it using the following guidelines.

Ask yourself these questions:

- Is my introductory sentence ("hook") interesting? *If it is not interesting to you, it certainly will not be interesting to the reader.*

- Does my thesis statement clearly state what my essay is about?

- Have I defined all technical terms and subject-specific vocabulary in my essay?

- Does each body paragraph have a clear topic sentence at the beginning that tells the reader exactly what the paragraph will be about? *Read each topic sentence without the rest of the paragraph to see if it can stand alone as a strong idea.*

- Does each of my topic sentences strongly support my thesis statement?

- Are there other concrete details, relevant facts, examples, quotations, graphics, or steps that I can add to help improve my explanation or help the reader to better follow my instructions?

- Are my sentences in a logical or practical order?

- Does each paragraph (except for the first) begin with an effective, relational transition?

- Are there other details that I can add as additional body paragraphs to create a fuller or clearer explanation?

- Are some of my sentences weak or confusing? Should they be removed because they do not help me to explain?

- Do my body paragraphs appear in the best possible order? Could I place them in a different order that is more logical or effective?

- Is each sentence constructed as well as it should be? *Read each sentence in each paragraph as if it were the only sentence on the page. This helps you to catch sentence fragments, run-on sentences, misspellings, and grammatical errors.*

- Does my concluding paragraph summarize and reinforce the ideas expressed in the essay? Have I written a powerful clincher?

Practice Use the Evaluation Form on the next page to evaluate the expository essay that you wrote for Lesson 20. Read your essay carefully as you check for the items listed on the Evaluation Form. Write YES or NO in the blank next to each question.

When you are finished, you will either be confident that you have a strong essay, or you will know where it needs to be improved.

If you answered NO to one or more of the questions on the Evaluation Form, rewrite to improve those areas.

When you can answer YES to every question on the Evaluation Form, you will have completed this assignment.

Expository Essay Evaluation Form

Thesis: _____

_____ Is my introductory sentence interesting? *If it is not interesting to you, it certainly will not be interesting to the reader.*

_____ Do I have a thesis statement that clearly explains the subject of this essay?

_____ Does my thesis statement clearly state my method of presentation?

_____ Does each body paragraph have a clear topic sentence at the beginning that tells the reader exactly what the paragraph will be about? *Read each topic sentence without the rest of the paragraph to see if it can stand alone as a strong idea.*

_____ Have I included every detail, fact, or example that I can to help improve my explanation and help the reader to better understand my point?

_____ Within each paragraph, are my sentences in a logical or practical order?

_____ Does each paragraph (except for the first paragraph) begin with an effective transition?

_____ Are there no other ideas that I can add as additional body paragraphs to create a fuller or clearer explanation?

_____ Are all of my sentences strong and clear? Do they all help me to explain?

_____ Do my body paragraphs appear in the best possible order? Is their order logical and effective?

_____ Is each sentence structured as well as it could be? *Read each sentence in each paragraph as if it were the only sentence on the page. This helps you to identify fragments, run-on sentences, and the overall strength or weakness of each sentence.*

_____ Does my concluding paragraph summarize and reinforce each main idea expressed in the essay? Is there a clincher sentence?

Preparing to Write a Personal Narrative

Personal Narrative Narrative writing tells a story or relates a series of events. In a **personal narrative,** the writer tells a story about a significant personal experience or event.

In this lesson, you will prepare to write a personal narrative in which you will share your feelings about how an experience affected you or taught you something. Your first-person account might include action, suspense, dialogue, and vivid description.

Choosing a Personal Experience To think of an experience for a personal narrative that you would like to share, consider the following:

- a wonderful (or disastrous) first time that you did something

- a memorable struggle or hardship that you experienced

- a "turning point" in your life

- an interesting, exciting, humorous, or moving event in your life

- an unusual or once-in-a-lifetime experience, such as touring a distant country, meeting a famous person, or making an amazing discovery

Reading through the daily journals that you have written might give you additional ideas.

Brainstorming On a piece of scratch paper, quickly write every experience that comes to your mind. When you have finished, select the one that you think is most interesting and write it on another piece of paper.

After selecting the experience that you plan to write about in your personal narrative, begin brainstorming to recall details or emotions about this experience. List all words and phrases that come to mind. Without concern for spelling or grammar, write everything that occurs to you.

Organizing Your Information Once you have gathered your thoughts and memories, begin to plan your narrative by organizing the events in a logical order, which might be chronological order, or the sequence in which the events occurred. Your rough plan might look something like this:

First: My sister and I were feeding our pets...

Then: We noticed that the rabbit was missing, and...

Then: Our friends helped us search, and...

Then: We saw some wild dogs, and...

Finally: We learned how important it is to keep the rabbit cage locked.

Practice For your personal narrative, write a rough plan similar to the one above. In the next lesson, you will expand each part of this plan into a paragraph and complete your narrative by filling in detail, action, and dialogue.

First: _____

_____

Then:_____

_____

Then: _____

_____

Then: _____

_____

Finally: _____

_____

_____

LESSON 23

Writing a Personal Narrative

In Lesson 22, you chose an interesting personal experience and created a rough plan for writing a personal narrative. In this lesson, you will use your rough plan and any other notes and begin writing your narrative.

Opening Paragraph   Remember that your opening paragraph should capture the interest of the reader and establish your tone, which reveals your feelings or attitudes about the experience. You will write in first person, using the pronoun *I* or *we.*

Body Paragraphs   Although you have a plan to follow, you may alter it as you write. Following the opening paragraph, each "then" part of your rough plan might become the topic sentence for a body paragraph in which you fill in details, actions, and any necessary dialogue.

Concluding Paragraph   Your concluding paragraph will include a personal summary or commentary about how the experience affected you or taught you something significant.

Practice   Write your personal narrative according to the guidelines above. Include an opening paragraph, two or more body paragraphs, and a concluding paragraph.

Evaluating the Personal Narrative

All of our writing is "work in progress." The knowledge that *writing is a process* guides our thinking throughout the construction of our personal narrative. From the first steps in selecting an experience to share, to organizing our thoughts, to creating body paragraphs, to adding transitions, we constantly make changes to improve our work.

Evaluating Your Writing

In Lesson 23, you completed your personal narrative. Now that some time has passed, you are ready to evaluate it using the following guidelines.

Ask yourself these questions:

- Is my introductory sentence interesting? *If it is not interesting to you, it certainly will not be interesting to the reader.*

- Does the beginning of the narrative clearly tell how I feel about the experience or event?

- Does each body paragraph have a clear topic sentence at the beginning that tells the reader exactly what the paragraph will be about? *Read each topic sentence without the rest of the paragraph to see if it can stand alone as a strong idea.*

- Is the first-person point of view consistently maintained throughout the narrative?

- Are there other details, descriptions, emotions, or dialogue I could add to make a more interesting narrative?

- Are my sentences in a logical or chronological order?

- Have I used a variety of time-related terms (transitions) to sequence (order) the events?

- Have I paced my essay appropriately?

- Does each paragraph (except for the first) begin with an effective transition?

- Are there other details that I can add as additional body paragraphs to create a fuller or more complete narrative?

- Are some of my sentences weak or confusing? Should they be removed because they do not relate to the story?

- Do my body paragraphs appear in the best possible order? Could I place them in a different order that is more logical or effective?

- Is each sentence constructed as well as it should be? *Read each sentence in each paragraph as if it were the only sentence on the page. This helps you to catch sentence fragments, run-on sentences, misspellings, and grammatical errors.*

- Does my concluding paragraph contain a summary or commentary about how the experience affected me?

Practice Use the Evaluation Form on the next page to evaluate the personal narrative that you wrote for Lesson 23. Read your narrative carefully as you check for the items listed on the Evaluation Form. Write YES or NO in the blank next to each question.

When you are finished, you will either be confident that you have a strong personal narrative, or you will know where it needs to be improved.

If you answered NO to one or more of the questions on the Evaluation Form, rewrite to improve those areas.

When you can answer YES to every question on the Evaluation Form, you will have completed this assignment.

Personal Narrative Evaluation Form

Title: _____

_____ Is my introductory sentence interesting? *If it is not interesting to you, it certainly won't be interesting to the reader.*

_____ Does the beginning of the narrative clearly tell how I feel about the experience or event?

_____ Is the first-person point of view consistently maintained throughout the narrative?

_____ Does each body paragraph have a clear topic sentence at the beginning that tells the reader exactly what the paragraph will be about? *Read each topic sentence without the rest of the paragraph to see if it can stand alone as a strong idea.*

_____ Do the details all contribute to the reader's understanding of my personal experience?

_____ Within each paragraph, are my sentences in a logical or practical order?

_____ Does each paragraph (except for the first paragraph) begin with an effective transition?

_____ Are there no other details that I can add as additional body paragraphs to create a fuller or more complete narrative?

_____ Are all of my sentences strong and clear? Do they all directly relate to the story?

_____ Do my body paragraphs appear in the best possible order? Is their order logical and effective?

_____ Is each sentence structured as well as it could be? *Read each sentence in each paragraph as if it were the only sentence on the page. This helps you to identify fragments, run-on sentences, and the overall strength or weakness of each sentence.*

_____ Does my concluding paragraph contain a personal summary or commentary about how the experience affected me or taught me something?

Preparing to Write a Descriptive Essay

Descriptive writing describes a person, place, object, or event. With language that appeals to the senses, descriptive writing creates pictures in the reader's mind. Strong, vivid, and precise words are essential in creating clear descriptions.

In this lesson, we shall discuss the use of modifiers, comparisons, and sensory expressions to create accurate and complete descriptions. Then you will prepare to write a descriptive essay about a person whom you can observe as you are writing.

Modifiers To add detail, we can use modifiers: adjectives and adverbs, phrases and clauses. Modifiers supply additional information, making nouns and verbs more specific and precise.

> *Humble, vigilant,* and *upright,* the banker *carefully* accounted for every penny.

Comparisons In addition to adding modifiers, we can use comparisons to make a description more vivid. *Simile* and *metaphor* are two kinds of comparisons. A *simile* expresses similarity between two things by using the word *like* or *as:*

> *Like* a rock, Lily remains stable even when everyone else goes crazy.

> Lily remains as stable *as* a rock.

A *metaphor*, on the other hand, describes one thing as though it were another thing:

> Lily is a *rock* in the midst of chaos.

Both types of comparison, simile and metaphor, help the reader to see a fuller picture of Lily.

Sensory Expressions To create a more vivid image, we can appeal to the reader's five senses by detailing things that one can see, hear, smell, taste, and touch. For example, we can hear an engine *rumble*, see a snowflake *glisten*, smell the *perfume* of a rose, feel the *scratchiness* of a wool sweater, and taste the *tart* apple that makes our lips pucker.

Below, Mary E. Wilkins Freeman describes Alma Way, the new leading soprano, in "A Village Singer."

> Now she fixed her large solemn blue eyes; her long, delicate face, which had been pretty, turned paler; the blue flowers on her bonnet trembled; her little thin gloved hands, clutching the singing book, shook perceptibly; but she sang out bravely.

Mary Wilkins's description demonstrates how a writer can use details, modifiers, and comparisons to give the reader a clear picture of a person. Circle each descriptive adjective.

In his novel *The Wind in the Willows*, Kenneth Grahame uses metaphor and sensory images to describe a river:

> —this *sleek, sinuous, full-bodied animal* [metaphor], chasing and chuckling, gripping things with a gurgle and leaving them with a laugh, to fling itself on fresh playmates that shook themselves free, and were caught and held again. All was a-shake and a-shiver—glints and gleams and sparkles, rustle and swirl, chatter and bubble.

In the same novel, the author goes on to describe in detail a room in the Badger's house:

> The Badger's winter stores, which indeed were visible everywhere, took up half the room—piles of apples, turnips, and potatoes, baskets full of nuts, and jars of honey; but the two little white beds on the remainder of the floor looked soft and inviting, and the linen on them, though coarse, was clean and smelt beautifully of lavender....

The examples above show how good authors create vivid pictures using details, modifiers, comparisons, and sensory expressions.

Brainstorming After choosing one person whom you can observe as you write, you are ready to begin brainstorming to gather precise and concrete details that will appeal to the reader's senses and fully describe that person.

You might want to consider these aspects of the person.

1. Physical appearance: size, age, gender; colors, shapes, and textures of hair, eyes, skin, and clothing; peculiar features or facial expressions; movements and gestures

2. Personality traits: mannerisms, habits, usual disposition. By their actions, people may demonstrate that they are intense or relaxed; hyperactive or laid-back; outgoing or shy; humble or proud; etc.

3. How the person affects others and the world around him or her: Where does the person live? What does the person do? What are his or her passions or interests? How does he

or she relate to others? How does this person make you or other people feel?

On a blank piece of paper, quickly write everything that comes to your mind concerning the person that you wish to describe. Without regard for spelling or grammar, write all the nouns, verbs, adjectives, adverbs, phrases, clauses, comparisons, and sensory expressions that occur to you.

Using Reference Materials

Use reference materials such as dictionaries and thesauruses, both print and digital, to find additional precise and appropriate words and phrases for your essay.

Recognizing Connotations

Connotations are the associations and emotions suggested by some words. A word's *denotation*, its literal, dictionary definition, is distinct from its *connotation*, which is its implied or suggested meaning. Although not all words have connotations, such words as *stingy, selfish, skinny, thin, race car*, and *jalopy* do.

Consider the word pairs below. Which word from each pair has a more positive connotation?

polished, completed　　　*fiction, fabrication*

faddish, fashionable　　　*food, feast*

We see that the words *polished, fiction, fashionable,* and *feast* have more positive connotations.

Consider the word pairs below. Which word from each pair has a more negative connotation?

passionate, violent　　　*gloat, rejoice*

devoted, henpecked　　　*substitute, sham*

We see that the words *violent, gloat, henpecked,* and *sham* have more negative connotations.

To choose the best words to convey our meaning, we must learn to recognize word connotations.

Organizing Your Information

Once you have gathered your thoughts and observations, begin to plan your descriptive essay by grouping the words and phrases into clusters. You might have one cluster of words and phrases that describe the person's physical appearance, another cluster focusing on the person's personality, and another telling about what the person does or how the person affects others and the world around him or her.

You can use each idea cluster to develop a topic sentence for each body paragraph in your essay.

Thesis Statement In your essay, you will be describing many different aspects of one person. What is the main impression you want your reader to receive concerning this person? Your thesis statement will sum up that which is most important.

Practice For your descriptive essay, write a thesis statement and three or more topic sentences about the person you wish to describe. In the next lesson, you will expand each topic sentence into a body paragraph by adding more detail. Keep your brainstorming paper and this assignment in your three-ring binder so that you will be ready to complete your essay.

THESIS STATEMENT: _____

_____

_____

Topic sentence: _____

_____

_____

Topic sentence: _____

_____

_____

Topic sentence: _____

_____

_____

LESSON 26

Writing a Descriptive Essay

In Lesson 25, you prepared to write your descriptive essay about a person of your choice. By brainstorming, you gathered ideas and details. Then you organized those details into clusters representing main ideas. From those clusters, you created a thesis statement and at least three topic sentences. Now you are ready to write the complete essay.

Practice Using the topic sentences that you wrote for Lesson 25, follow the steps below to complete the descriptive essay.

1. Expand each topic sentence into a body paragraph, keeping your thesis in mind. Refer to your brainstorming notes and idea clusters to write body sentences that add more detail and create a vivid picture in the reader's mind.

2. Create an introductory paragraph and a concluding paragraph. Remember that the introductory sentence should grab the reader's interest and that the "last words" of your conclusion will leave a lasting impression.

3. Add a variety of transitions between body paragraphs to make your ideas easier for the reader to follow. Pay special attention to the transition into the concluding paragraph.

4. Finally, put all the parts together to form a complete essay. As you are working, make any necessary corrections to your previous work. You might add things, delete things, or make any other change that results in a clearer, fuller descriptive essay.

Additional Practice (Optional) After you have evaluated your descriptive essay using the guidelines in Lesson 27, you might try writing another descriptive essay on a topic of your choice or on one of these topics:

1. A character from a novel you have read

2. A room in your house or apartment

3. A pet, or an animal that interests you

4. An interesting or beautiful outdoor scene

5. A sporting event, birthday party, or other kind of celebration

Evaluating the Descriptive Essay

Because *writing is a process* and all of our writing is "work in progress," we constantly make changes to improve our work.

Evaluating Your Writing

In Lesson 26, you completed your descriptive essay. Now that some time has passed, you are ready to evaluate it using the following guidelines.

Ask yourself these questions:

- Is my introductory sentence interesting? *If it is not interesting to you, it certainly will not be interesting to the reader.*

- Does the thesis statement focus on a single person, place, object, or event?

- Does the thesis statement give my main impression of the person, place, object, or event that I am describing?

- Does each body paragraph have a clear topic sentence at the beginning that tells the reader exactly what the paragraph will be about? *Read each topic sentence without the rest of the paragraph to see if it can stand alone as a strong idea.*

- Are there other details, modifiers, comparisons, or sensory expressions I could add to help the reader to visualize my topic?

- Are my sentences in a logical order?

- Does each paragraph (except for the first) begin with an effective transition?

- Are there other details that I can add as additional body paragraphs to create a fuller or more complete description?

- Are some of my sentences weak or confusing? Should they be removed because they do not relate to the topic?

- Do my body paragraphs appear in the best possible order? Could I place them in a different order that is more logical or effective?

- Is each sentence constructed as well as it should be? *Read each sentence in each paragraph as if it were the only sentence on the page. This helps you to catch sentence fragments, run-on sentences, misspellings, and grammatical errors.*

- Does my concluding paragraph sum up my main impression of the person, place, object, or event?

Practice   Use the Evaluation Form on the next page to evaluate the descriptive essay that you wrote for Lesson 26. Read your descriptive essay carefully as you check for the items listed on the Evaluation Form. Write YES or NO in the blank next to each question.

When you are finished, you will either be confident that you have a strong descriptive essay, or you will know where it needs to be improved.

If you answered NO to one or more of the questions on the Evaluation Form, rewrite to improve those areas.

When you can answer YES to every question on the Evaluation Form, you will have completed this assignment.

Descriptive Essay Evaluation Form

Topic: _____

_____ Is my introductory sentence interesting? *If it is not interesting to you, it certainly won't be interesting to the reader.*

_____ Does the thesis statement focus on a single person, place, object, or event?

_____ Does the thesis statement give my main impression of that person, place, object, or event?

_____ Does each body paragraph have a clear topic sentence at the beginning that tells the reader exactly what the paragraph will be about? *Read each topic sentence without the rest of the paragraph to see if it can stand alone as a strong idea.*

_____ Do the details all contribute to the reader's ability to visualize or mentally experience my topic?

_____ Within each paragraph, are my sentences in a logical order?

_____ Does each paragraph (except for the first paragraph) begin with an effective transition?

_____ Have I used enough modifiers, comparisons, and sensory expressions to enable the reader to visualize my topic?

_____ Are all of my sentences strong and clear? Do they all directly relate to the topic?

_____ Do my body paragraphs appear in the best possible order? Is their order logical and effective?

_____ Is each sentence structured as well as it could be? *Read each sentence in each paragraph as if it were the only sentence on the page. This helps you to identify fragments, run-on sentences, and the overall strength or weakness of each sentence.*

_____ Does my concluding paragraph sum up my main impression of my topic?

LESSON 28

Writing a Chapter Summary

A summary is a brief restatement of the main ideas in something one has read. In a summary, the writer leaves out details, condensing a long passage—a whole story, chapter, or book—to its main ideas. Therefore, the summary is much shorter than the original passage.

In this lesson, we shall practice writing a one-paragraph summary of a chapter in a novel.

Chapter Summary If you were reading a novel to a friend, and if your friend fell asleep during one of the chapters, he or she might miss a great deal of the action or storyline. Your brief *summary* of that missing chapter could help your friend to go on quickly to the next chapter without confusion and without rereading the entire chapter.

Example Below is a summary of the first chapter in *The Prince and the Pauper* by Mark Twain. Notice that verbs are present tense.

> On an autumn day in London during the early 1500s, two boys are born—Tom Canty and Edward Tudor. Tom Canty, born to poor parents, is unwanted. On the other hand, Edward Tudor is the long-awaited child of a rich and powerful family. All of England celebrates his birth with feasting, dancing, bonfires, and parades. While little Tom lies in rags, Edward rests in a lavish crib surrounded by silks and satins. Although the two boys are born on the same day in the same town, their circumstances could not be more different.

Practice In a single paragraph, summarize one chapter of a novel that you are reading or have read in the past (or a novel from the list below). Your paragraph should not exceed eight sentences. Your summary should include major characters and provide a sense of what happens in the chapter. Use present tense.

Suggested novels for this exercise:

The Adventures of Tom Sawyer, by Mark Twain

Little House on the Prairie, by Laura Ingalls Wilder

Little Women, by Louisa May Alcott

Dr. Jekyll and Mr. Hyde, by Robert Louis Stevenson

The Lion, the Witch, and the Wardrobe, by C.S. Lewis

Writing a Short Story Summary

We have learned that a summary condenses a longer passage to a shorter one, leaving out details and giving only the main ideas of the original passage.

In this lesson, we shall practice writing a one-paragraph summary of a short story.

Short Story Summary
If you had read an interesting short story and wanted to tell a friend about it, you might give your friend a *summary* of the story. You would not tell the *whole* story or give away the ending. Instead, you would summarize, giving some general information about the main characters, setting, and major conflict.

Example
Below is a summary of the short story "Kitterwick Cottage" by Nancy Hoven. Notice that verbs are present tense.

> "Kitterwick Cottage" is an entertaining short story about a remarkable species of kitty-cats known as Kitterwicks. Legends abound concerning these elusive, mysterious creatures who live in their own secret society, hidden from humankind. The main character, Little Noosh, has come of age and now must embark on the greatest experience of his life—finding a job—which isn't easy with his odd, over-sized, extra-toed paws and a propensity towards clumsiness and cluelessness. Little Noosh is joined on his journey by a host of delightfully eccentric characters and driven to distraction by a series of madcap misadventures. Along the way, he learns some of life's lessons, the most important being that with hard work, a positive attitude, and persistence, dreams really do come true.

Practice
Write a one-paragraph summary of the personal narrative that you wrote for Lesson 23. Your paragraph should not exceed eight sentences. Your summary should include general information about *what* happened, *who* was involved, and *where* the action took place. Use present tense of verbs.

Additional Practice
Read one of the short stories or books suggested on the next page or one that your teacher suggests. Then write a one-paragraph summary of the story or book. Your paragraph should not exceed eight sentences. Your summary should include general information about main characters, setting, and plot.

Suggested reading:

"The Cricket on the Hearth," by Charles Dickens

"Old Yeller," by Fred Gipson

"The Legend of Sleepy Hollow," by Washington Irving

"The Notorious Jumping Frog of Calaveras County,"
by Mark Twain

"The Mysterious Island," by Jules Verne

Developing an Outline

An outline can help us to organize our ideas. In an outline, we can arrange and sequence thoughts in a logical manner.

In this lesson, we shall look at the basic outline form and practice developing an outline from an essay that we have already written. This exercise will give us confidence in our ability to make an outline in preparation for writing future essays or research papers.

Outline Form An outline is a list of topics and subtopics arranged in an organized form. We use Roman numerals for main topics. For subtopics, we use uppercase letters. For a very detailed outline, we use alternating numbers and letters as shown below.

Title

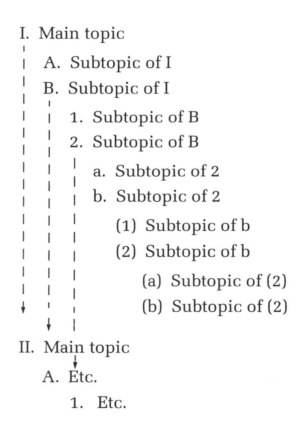

I. Main topic
   A. Subtopic of I
   B. Subtopic of I
      1. Subtopic of B
      2. Subtopic of B
         a. Subtopic of 2
         b. Subtopic of 2
            (1) Subtopic of b
            (2) Subtopic of b
               (a) Subtopic of (2)
               (b) Subtopic of (2)

II. Main topic
   A. Etc.
      1. Etc.

Notice that we indent subtopics so that all letters or numbers of the same kind will come directly under one another in a vertical line. Notice also that we use at least **two subdivisions** (letters or numbers of the same kind) for a category.

Topic Outline An outline may be either a topic outline or a sentence outline. In a **topic outline,** each main topic or subtopic is written as a single word or phrase. Below is an example of a topic outline of the first part of an essay on eating vegetables.

The Great Vegetable Debate

I. Why eating vegetables is necessary

    A. To nourish the body

    B. To prevent disease

II. Why some people do not like vegetables

    A. Bitter taste

    B. Slimy texture

Sentence Outline In a **sentence outline,** each topic is expressed as a complete sentence. Notice how the sentence outline below communicates more meaning than the short phrases of the topic outline.

The Great Vegetable Debate

I. Eating vegetables is necessary.

    A. We must eat vegetables to nourish the body.

    B. Certain vegetables can help prevent disease.

II. Some people do not like to eat vegetables.

    A. Many vegetables have a bitter taste.

    B. Some cooked vegetables are slimy in texture.

Practice On a separate sheet of paper, practice the outlining process by organizing the following set of information in a topic outline form:

Main topic: Forms of Money

Subtopics: Bills
          Checks
          Coins

Sub-subtopics: Pennies	Traveler's checks
$5 bills	$1 bills
Quarters	Nickels
$20 bills	Dimes
Personal checks	$10 bills

Additional Practice For Lesson 16, you wrote a persuasive essay containing at least three body paragraphs. Create a topic outline covering the body paragraphs of that essay. (Hint: The topic sentence of each body paragraph will become a word or phrase beside a Roman numeral indicating a main topic in your outline. Therefore, your outline will have at least three Roman numerals.)

Additional Practice (Optional) For Lesson 26, you wrote a descriptive essay containing at least three body paragraphs. Create a topic outline for this essay.

Preparing to Write a Research Paper: The Working Bibliography

A research paper is a type of expository writing based on information gathered from a variety of reliable sources. In the future, you may be asked to write a research paper for an English, history, science, art, or music class. Knowing the procedure for writing a good research paper will help you to become a successful high school and college student.

In this lesson, we shall learn how to prepare for writing a research paper on an assigned subject. To practice the procedure, you may choose one of the following subjects:

1. The Platypus, an Unusual Mammal

2. What Causes Tornadoes

3. The Building of the Panama Canal

4. How the Grand Canyon Was Formed

5. A subject suggested by your teacher

Tone The research paper requires a serious tone. The writing should be formal and impersonal. Therefore, we do not use first person pronouns, such as *I, me,* or *my.*

Gathering Sources of Information The first step in researching your subject is to compile a **working bibliography,** a collection of possible sources of information. Consider the following possibilities for your research:

• library research aids including card catalog, *Readers' Guide,* and reference works

• Internet

• Google Scholar

• government publications

• personal interviews or correspondence

• museums

• scholarly journals

Evaluating Sources of Information

Not all sources are reliable or useful. We must evaluate each source for its usefulness. Asking the following questions will help us to evaluate each source.

1. *Is the information current?* A 1970 study of smog in large cities is out-of-date. Therefore, it would not be an appropriate source for a paper on today's pollution problems.

2. *Is the source objective and impartial?* An article written by the president of Mountain Spring Bottled Water about impurities in local well water might not be an objective source. The author could be trying to sell you something.

3. *For what audience was the source intended?* Material written for young children might be over-simplified, while material written for specialists might be too technical.

Preparing Bibliography Cards

After gathering sources, evaluating each one for its usefulness, and choosing only those that are appropriate, we are ready to compile a working bibliography, the list of sources from which we will glean information for our research paper. Using three-inch by five-inch index cards, we record each source on a separate card. We include all the information listed below and on the next page, for we will need it to prepare our final bibliography when our paper is completed.

BOOKS

1. Author's (or editor's) full name, last name first. Indicate editor by placing *ed.* after the name. If the book has more than one author, only the first author is written last name first. Others are written first name first.

2. Title and subtitle underlined

3. City of publication

4. Publisher's name

5. Most recent copyright year

MAGAZINE, NEWSPAPER, JOURNAL, AND ENCYCLOPEDIA ARTICLES

1. Author's (or editor's) full name, last name first. Indicate editor by placing *ed.* after the name. If the article has more

than one author, only the first author is written last name first. Others are written first name first.

2. Title of article in quotation marks

3. Name of magazine, newspaper, journal, or encyclopedia underlined

4. Date and page numbers of *magazines*

   Date, edition, section, page numbers of *newspapers*

   Volume, year, page numbers of *journals*
   Edition and year of *encyclopedias*

ELECTRONIC SOURCES

1. Author's (or editor's) full name, last name first. Indicate editor by placing *ed.* after the name. If the article has more than one author, only the first author is written last name first. Others are written first name first.

2. Title of article in quotation marks

3. Books, magazines, newspapers, journals, encyclopedias, or Web sites underlined

4. Date and page numbers of magazines

   Date, edition, section, page numbers of newspapers.

   Volume, year, page numbers of journals

   Edition and year of encyclopedias

   City of publication, publisher's name, and most recent copyright year of books

5. The date that you accessed the source

6. The URL in angle brackets

We assign each bibliography card a "source number" and write it in the upper left corner. Later we will use this number to identify the sources of our notes. Below are some sample bibliography cards.

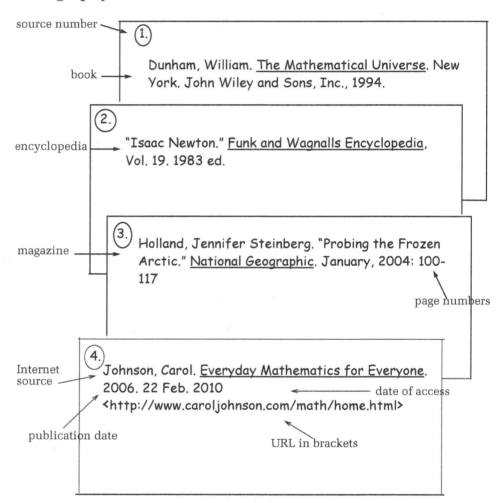

source number
① 1.
book → Dunham, William. The Mathematical Universe. New York. John Wiley and Sons, Inc., 1994.

② 2.
encyclopedia → "Isaac Newton." Funk and Wagnalls Encyclopedia, Vol. 19. 1983 ed.

③ 3.
magazine → Holland, Jennifer Steinberg. "Probing the Frozen Arctic." National Geographic. January, 2004: 100-117
page numbers

④ 4.
Internet source → Johnson, Carol. Everyday Mathematics for Everyone. 2006. 22 Feb. 2010 ← date of access
<http://www.caroljohnson.com/math/home.html>
publication date
URL in brackets

Practice After you have chosen a subject from the list of suggestions for your research paper, follow the instructions in this lesson for gathering and evaluating sources and for preparing bibliography cards. Locate at least four appropriate sources and prepare a bibliography card for each one. Remember to assign each card a source number and write it in the upper left corner.

LESSON 32

Preparing to Write a Research Paper: Notes, Thesis, Outline

In Lesson 31, you chose a subject for a research paper and created a working bibliography, at least four sources of information that you will use for your paper. In this lesson, you will take notes from these sources, organize your notes, create a thesis statement, and develop an outline for your paper.

Taking Notes It is helpful to use four-inch by six-inch index cards for taking notes. As you read through your sources, write down information that applies to your subject. Write most of your notes in your own words. You may summarize the author's main ideas, or you may record specific facts or details in your own words. If you quote the author, you must enclose the author's exact words in quotation marks.

Whenever you take notes from a source, you must credit that source whether you quote an author or use your own words. Do not *plagiarize*, or use another person's words or ideas without acknowledging the source.

In the upper right corner of your note card, you will enter the source number from your working bibliography.

At the end of each note, write the page or pages on which you found the information.

Below is a sample note card.

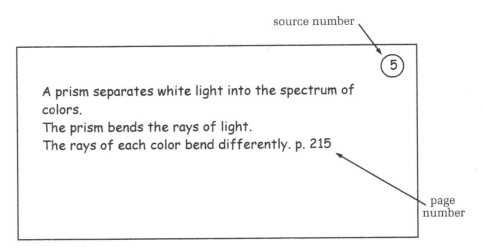

source number

⑤

A prism separates white light into the spectrum of colors.
The prism bends the rays of light.
The rays of each color bend differently. p. 215

page number

Organizing Your Information After you have taken notes on all your sources and gathered sufficient information for your research paper, take some time to organize your note cards and arrange them in a logical order.

Thesis Statement Now look over your organized notes and write a thesis statement that clearly explains the main idea of your research paper.

Outline In Lesson 30, you learned to develop an outline. Use your organized note cards to help you create an informal topic outline for your research paper. This outline will guide you as you begin to write the first draft of your paper in the next lesson.

Practice Follow the instructions in this lesson for taking notes from your sources. Then organize your notes, write a thesis statement, and develop an outline for your research paper.

LESSON 33

Writing the Research Paper

In Lesson 32, you took notes from your sources, organized your notes, wrote a thesis statement, and created an outline for your research paper.

Writing the First Draft

With your outline, your thesis statement, your notes, and your bibliography cards in front of you, you are ready to begin writing the first draft of your research paper. A first draft is a rough copy that is for your use only. It is meant to be revised again and again until you are satisfied with it.

As you write, keep in mind your thesis statement, your purpose, and the need for a formal tone. Use the information on your note cards to support your thesis and to fill in the details as you follow your outline for organization.

Create an opening paragraph that captures the reader's attention. Consider beginning with an interesting statement, an anecdote, or an example. Make certain that your opening paragraph includes your thesis statement.

Use the main points in your outline to create topic sentences for your body paragraphs. Then expand these topic sentences into paragraphs, making sure that all of your information relates to your thesis statement.

Pay special attention to transitions as you begin each new paragraph.

Your concluding paragraph will summarize and reinforce the ideas set forth in the rest of your research paper.

Documentation of Sources

Writing the first draft of a research paper involves bringing together information from your different sources, which you must acknowledge properly. We call this **documentation of sources.**

As you write, you must credit your sources for both ideas and quotations. There are various methods of documenting sources for research papers. In this book, we shall practice a method called *parenthetical citations.* This form identifies sources in parentheses that are placed as close as possible to the ideas or quotations that we cite.

Inside the parentheses, we place a reference to the source on our bibliography card. Usually, the reference inside the parentheses consists only of an author's last name and page number from which the material was taken.

For example, (Smith 31) would appear right after an idea taken from page thirty-one in Albert Smith's book.

When no author and only a title is given for a source, we place a shortened form of the title and the page number or numbers in the parentheses: ("Fly in the Ointment" 110-111).

In the example below, notice that the end punctuation for a sentence containing borrowed material is placed *after* the parenthetical citation.

> Charles Dickens invented clever nicknames such as "the Artful Dodger" (Smith 31). ⟵ punctuation mark

The highly respected Modern Language Association (MLA) gives us many more detailed guidelines for parenthetical citations. However, in this lesson, we shall follow the simplified instructions above.

The Bibliography   The bibliography, the list of the sources that you used as you wrote your paper, comes at the end of the research paper.

Follow these steps to create your bibliography:

1. Alphabetize your bibliography cards according to the last names of the authors or the first important word in a title if there is no author.

2. Copy the information from all of your alphabetized bibliography cards under the title "Bibliography" or "Works Cited."

3. Indent all lines after the first line of each entry and punctuate as shown in the example below.

Works Cited

Grim, Edmund. "Six Ways to Clean the Sewer." Home and Grounds Journal, July, 1999: 12-15.

Leadfoot, Doris. A Study in Dynamics. New York, Grassvale Publishers, 2001.

In high school and college, you will learn to follow more detailed guidelines for bibliographic entries. However, in this lesson you may follow the simplified instructions given unless your teacher advises you to do otherwise.

Practice Follow the procedure given in this lesson for writing the first draft of your research paper and for creating your bibliography, or list of works cited.

LESSON 34

Evaluating the Research Paper

The knowledge that *writing is a process* guides our thinking throughout the construction of our research paper. From the first steps in choosing our subject, to gathering information and organizing our thoughts, to creating body paragraphs, to adding transitions, we constantly make changes to improve our work.

Evaluating Your Writing

In Lesson 33, you completed the first draft of your research paper. Now that some time has passed, you are ready to evaluate it using the following guidelines.

Ask yourself these questions:

- Is my introductory sentence interesting? *If it is not interesting to you, it certainly will not be interesting to the reader.*

- Does my thesis clearly state the purpose of my paper?

- Does the beginning of the research paper clearly establish a formal, serious tone?

- Does each body paragraph have a clear topic sentence at the beginning that tells the reader exactly what the paragraph will be about? *Read each topic sentence without the rest of the paragraph to see if it can stand alone as a strong idea.*

- Does each paragraph include specific details and examples from my research?

- Have I given proper credit for each piece of borrowed information?

- Are my sentences in a logical order?

- Does each paragraph (except for the first) begin with an effective transition?

- Are there other details that I can add as additional body paragraphs to create a fuller or more complete paper?

- Are some of my sentences weak or confusing? Should they be removed because they do not relate to my thesis?

- Do my body paragraphs appear in the best possible order? Could I place them in a different order that is more logical or effective?

- Is each sentence constructed as well as it should be? *Read each sentence in each paragraph as if it were the only sentence on the page. This helps you to catch sentence fragments, run-on sentences, misspellings, and grammatical errors.*

- Does my ending paragraph obviously conclude my presentation? Does it reinforce my thesis statement?

- Are my sources reliable, objective, and current?

Practice Use the Evaluation Form on the next page to evaluate the research paper you wrote for Lesson 33. Read your research paper carefully as you check for the items listed on the Evaluation Form. Write YES or NO in the blank next to each question.

When you are finished, you will either be confident that you have a strong research paper, or you will know where it needs to be improved.

If you answered NO to one or more of the questions on the Evaluation Form, rewrite to improve those areas.

When you can answer YES to every question on the Evaluation Form, you will have completed this assignment.

Research Paper Evaluation Form

Subject: _____

_____ Is my introductory sentence interesting? *If it is not interesting to you, it certainly will not be interesting to the reader.*

_____ Does the beginning of the research paper clearly establish a formal, serious tone?

_____ Does the thesis clearly state the purpose of the paper?

_____ Does each body paragraph have a clear topic sentence at the beginning that tells the reader exactly what the paragraph will be about? *Read each topic sentence without the rest of the paragraph to see if it can stand alone as a strong idea.*

_____ Do the details all contribute to the reader's understanding of the thesis?

_____ Within each paragraph, are my sentences in a logical or practical order?

_____ Does each paragraph (except for the first paragraph) begin with an effective transition?

_____ Is each piece of borrowed material given proper credit?

_____ Are all of my sentences strong and clear? Do they all directly relate to the thesis?

_____ Do my body paragraphs appear in the best possible order? Is their order logical and effective?

_____ Is each sentence structured as well as it could be? *Read each sentence in each paragraph as if it were the only sentence on the page. This helps you to identify fragments, run-on sentences, and the overall strength or weakness of each sentence.*

_____ Does my concluding paragraph summarize my research and reinforce my thesis statement?

_____ Are my sources reliable, objective, and current?

Preparing to Write
an Imaginative Story

We have practiced writing vivid descriptions of people, places, objects, or events using details, modifiers, comparisons, and sensory expressions. We have also written a personal narrative with dialogue, logical sentence order, and effective transitions. In this lesson, we shall use all the writing skills we have learned so far to create our own imaginative story.

An imaginative story is fiction; it is not a true story, although it may be based on something that really happened.

Conflict, characters, setting, and plot are all parts of the imaginative story. In preparing to write our story, we shall gather information concerning each of these parts.

Conflict A short story must have a problem or situation in which struggle occurs. A character may be in conflict with another character, with the forces of nature, with the rules of society, or even with his or her own self, as an internal conflict brought about by pangs of conscience or feelings of confusion.

For example, notice the possible conflicts related to the two situations below.

SITUATION 1: Iona does not like her middle name
and wants to change it.

Conflict: Some people tease her about her name.

Conflict: Iona's parents gave her that name and
do not want her to change it.

Conflict: Iona's grandma feels hurt, for Iona was
named after her.

SITUATION 2: Ivan forgets to set his alarm clock to
wake him for his basketball game.

Conflict: He does not have time to eat breakfast,
so he might not have energy to play
his best in the game.

Conflict: He has missed the bus and does not know
how he will get to the game.

Conflict: His team might have to forfeit the game,

for they will not have enough players.

To find a situation and conflict for your own imaginative story, you might talk to friends or family members, watch the news, read the newspaper, or observe what is happening in the lives of people around you.

In preparation for story writing, spend several minutes brainstorming with the help of a friend, teacher, or family member to gather ideas of situations and conflicts. Write down all the situations and possible resulting conflicts that come to mind. Then choose the one conflict that most interests you for your imaginative story.

Tone Your attitude toward the conflict will create the **tone** of your story. The details and language that you use might evoke joy, fear, amusement, grief, or some other emotion. For example, you will want your story to make the reader laugh if you feel that the situation facing the characters is funny. On the other hand, if you feel that the situation is serious and worrisome, you will try to increase the reader's anxiety.

After choosing your conflict, plan how you will establish the tone of your story by answering the following questions:

1. What is my attitude toward the conflict and the characters involved in it?

2. What details can I use to create this mood, or evoke these emotions, in the reader?

Point of View You may tell your story from either the first-person or third-person point of view.

In the first-person point of view, the story is narrated, using the pronoun *I*, by one person who either participates in or witnesses the conflict. Only the narrator's thoughts are expressed, as in the example below.

> *Charles stuffed a mysterious envelope into my hand and left without an explanation.*

In the third-person, or omniscient, point of view, the story is narrated by someone outside the story, someone who knows everything—each character's thoughts and actions. This allows the writer to reveal what any character thinks or does, as in the example on the next page.

Somewhat embarrassed, Charles just stuffed the Valentine into Margaret's hand and walked away without a word.

Before you begin writing your imaginative story, you must choose an appropriate point of view from which to tell about the conflict.

Characters   To create a captivating story, you must develop interesting and believable characters. Engaged in a struggle, the main character, or *protagonist*, might be opposed by another character, an *antagonist*. There may be other characters as well.

As you develop your characters, attempt to keep them consistent in their behavior and show logical reasons for any change in their behavior. For example, if an ordinarily greedy character suddenly acts generously, you must explain why.

Invent your characters by noting their physical appearance, actions, and personality traits.

Dialogue   Dialogue is the spoken words of characters. A character's words can reveal things about the character's personality, background, thoughts, and attitudes. You can use dialogue to develop your characters and make your story more interesting.

Spend a few minutes brainstorming in order to gather ideas about your main characters. Give each one a name, some physical attributes, and a distinctive personality.

Setting   The setting is the time and place of the action. Vivid, specific details help to describe the setting of a story. You must consider both location and time. Does your story take place indoors, in a specific room, or outdoors, on a mountain, beach, or prairie? Or, does it take place on an airplane, boat, or train? Do the events occur in the morning, afternoon, or evening? Does the story happen in the past, present, or future?

Decide where and when your story will take place and jot down a few details that you can use later to describe your setting.

Plot The plot is the action of your story. Once you have chosen a conflict, one or more characters, and the setting of your story, you are ready to develop the action using this story plan:

BEGINNING OF STORY

Present your characters.

Establish the setting and tone.

Introduce the conflict.

MIDDLE OF STORY

List a series of actions that build to a climax.

END OF STORY

Resolve the conflict or show why it cannot be resolved.

Use the plan above to make notes, which you can expand later into a full imaginative story.

Practice Follow the instructions in this lesson for brainstorming, choosing a conflict, deciding on the tone and point of view, inventing characters, describing the setting, and planning the plot of your imaginative story. On a separate piece of paper, answer the following questions:

1. Who are your characters? Give a brief description of each.

2. What is the setting? Give the time and place.

3. Describe the tone, the emotions the reader will experience.

4. What is the conflict?

5. Briefly list some actions that will build to a climax.

6. How will you resolve the conflict?

Keep your answers to these questions in your three-ring binder. In the next lesson, you will use this information as you write your imaginative story.

LESSON 36

Writing an Imaginative Story

In Lesson 35, you prepared to write your imaginative story. By brainstorming, you gathered ideas and details. You chose a conflict, you decided on the tone and point of view, you invented characters, you described your setting, and you roughly planned the plot. Now you are ready to write the imaginative story.

Keep this plan in front of you as you write:

BEGINNING OF STORY

Present your characters.

Establish the setting and tone.

Introduce the conflict.

MIDDLE OF STORY

List a series of actions that build to a climax.

END OF STORY

Resolve the conflict.

Practice Using your notes from Lesson 35 and the plan above, follow the steps below to write your story.

1. Write an introductory sentence ("hook") that will grab the reader's attention.

2. At the beginning of the story, in whatever order you think is best, establish the setting and tone, present your characters, and introduce the conflict.

3. Add dialogue to reveal more about your characters' personalities, thoughts, and motivations.

4. Keep the point of view consistent throughout the story.

5. Write a series of actions that build to a climax.

6. Resolve the conflict at the end of your story.

LESSON 37

Evaluating the Imaginative Story

Because *writing is a process* and all of our writing is "work in progress," we constantly make changes to improve our work. This is especially true when writing an imaginative story. As you create your story, you may see opportunities for revisiting previous parts of your story to add more or different traits to a character or to alter his or her actions.

Evaluating Your Writing

In Lesson 36, you completed your imaginative story. Now that some time has passed, you are ready to evaluate it using the following guidelines.

Ask yourself these questions:

- Does my introductory sentence ("hook") capture the reader's attention?

- Does the beginning of the story establish the tone and suggest the conflict?

- Are the characters believable and interesting?

- Have I revealed the characters' personalities and motivations through dialogue and action as well as description?

- Are my characters consistent in their behavior? Have I adequately explained any changes from their normal behavior?

- Are there other details, modifiers, comparisons, or sensory expressions I could add to help the reader to visualize the setting?

- Do the actions flow logically from one to another?

- Do the actions build suspense?

- Does the dialogue sound natural?

- Does the point of view remain constant throughout the story?

- Are some of my sentences weak or confusing? Should any be removed because they do not relate to the story?

- Do my sentences appear in the best possible order? Could I place them in a more logical or effective order?

- Is each sentence constructed as well as it should be? *Read each sentence in each paragraph as if it were the only sentence on the page. This helps you to catch sentence fragments, run-on sentences, misspellings, and grammatical errors.*

- Is the end of the story believable and satisfying? Has the conflict been resolved, or have you shown why it cannot be resolved?

Practice Use the Evaluation Form on the next page to evaluate the imaginative story you wrote for Lesson 36. Read your story carefully as you check for the items listed on the Evaluation Form. Write YES or NO in the blank next to each question.

When you are finished, you will either be confident that you have a strong imaginative story, or you will know where it needs to be improved.

If you answered NO to one or more of the questions on the Evaluation Form, rewrite to improve those areas.

When you can answer YES to every question on the Evaluation Form, you will have completed this assignment.

Imaginative Story Evaluation Form

Title: _____

_____ Does my introductory sentence ("hook") capture the reader's attention?

_____ Does the beginning of the story establish the tone and suggest the conflict?

_____ Are the characters believable and interesting?

_____ Have I revealed the characters' personalities and motivations through dialogue and action as well as description?

_____ Are my characters consistent in their behavior? Have I adequately explained any change from their normal behavior?

_____ Have I included sufficient details, modifiers, comparisons, and sensory expressions to enable the reader to visualize the setting?

_____ Do the actions flow logically from one to another?

_____ Do the actions build suspense?

_____ Does the dialogue sound natural?

_____ Does the point of view remain consistent throughout the story?

_____ Is each sentence strong and clear? Does each sentence relate to the story?

_____ Is each sentence structured as well as it could be? *Read each sentence in each paragraph as if it were the only sentence on the page. This helps you to identify fragments, run-on sentences, and the overall strength or weakness of each sentence.*

_____ Is the end of the story believable and satisfying? Has the conflict been resolved?

Writing in Response to Literature

We read many books for pleasure; however, there are times when we are expected to analyze and reflect on what we read. This is called active reading. In active reading, you ask yourself what kind of text you are reading. Is it fictional? an essay? an editorial? Then you decide on the author's purpose. Is it to entertain, inform, or persuade? Next you pinpoint the main idea, or find the thesis. Finally, you find evidence in the text to support your thoughts about the main idea or thesis.

When we write about literature, we use the present tense of verbs, as in the sentence below.

Beth eagerly *volunteers* to help.

In this lesson, we shall examine characters from the well-known novel *Little Women.*

Carefully read the following excerpt from Chapter 2, "A Merry Christmas," of *Little Women*:

"Merry Christmas, little daughters! I'm glad you began at once, and hope you will keep on. But I want to say one word before we sit down. Not far away from here lies a poor woman with a little newborn baby. Six children are huddled into one bed to keep from freezing, for they have no fire. There is nothing to eat over there, and the oldest boy came to tell me that they were suffering hunger and cold. My girls, will you give them your breakfast as a Christmas present?"

They were all unusually hungry, having waited nearly an hour, and for a minute no one spoke, only a minute, for Jo exclaimed impetuously, "I'm so glad you came before we began!"

"May I go and help carry the things to the poor little children?" asked Beth eagerly.

"I shall take the cream and the muffings," added Amy, heroically giving up the article she most liked.

Meg was already covering the buckwheats, and piling the bread into one big plate.

"I thought you'd do it," said Mrs. March, smiling as if satisfied. "You shall all go and help me, and when we come back we will have bread and milk for breakfast, and make it up at dinnertime."

They were soon ready, and the procession set out. Fortunately it was early, and they went through back streets, so few people saw them, and no one laughed at the queer party.

A poor, bare, miserable room it was, with broken windows, no fire, ragged bedclothes, a sick mother, wailing baby, and a group of pale, hungry children cuddled under one old quilt, trying to keep warm.

How the big eyes stared and the blue lips smiled as the girls went in.

"Ach, mein Gott! It is good angels come to us!" said the poor woman, crying for joy.

"Funny angels in hoods and mittens," said Jo, and set them to laughing.

In a few minutes, it really did seem as if kind spirits had been at work there. Hannah, who had carried wood, made a fire, and stopped up the broken panes with old hats and her own cloak. Mrs. March gave the mother tea and gruel, and comforted her with promises of help, while she dressed the little baby as tenderly as if it had been her own. The girls meantime spread the table, set the children round the fire, and fed them like so many hungry birds, laughing, talking, and trying to understand the funny broken English.

"Das ist gut!" "Die Engel-kinder!" cried the poor things as they ate and warmed their purple hands at the comfortable blaze. The girls had never been called angel children before, and thought it very agreeable, especially Jo, who had been considered a 'Sancha' ever since she was born. That was a very happy breakfast, though they didn't get any of it. And when they went away, leaving comfort behind, I think there were not in all the city four merrier people than the hungry little girls who gave away their breakfasts and contented themselves with bread and milk on Christmas morning.

"That's loving our neighbor better than ourselves, and I like it," said Meg, as they set out their presents while their mother was upstairs collecting clothes for the poor Hummels.

Practice Answer the following questions about the excerpt above. You may work independently, with your teacher, or with other classmates. Remember to use the present tense of verbs.

1. Why does Mrs. March describe the Hummel Family in such detail to her daughters? What are these details?

2. "For a minute, no one spoke..." Why does a minute pass before anyone responds to Mrs. March's description and plea?

3. Why do you think that Mrs. March is approached for help? What does this tell you about her? What actions prove her compassionate heart?

4. What does the reader know about Jo?

5. What does the reader know about Meg? Cite lines from the excerpt.

6. How does the reader know that Amy struggles with sacrificing her Christmas breakfast?

7. What does the reader learn about Beth?

8. How does the reader know that the girls enjoy sharing their Christmas breakfast?

9. What figures of speech does the author use? Cite one and explain its meaning.

10. In another book, magazine, newspaper, or online source, find a story or poem with a similar theme to the one in this passage. Explain how the story or poem relates to this passage.

After answering the questions above, compare your answers with those in the Teacher Guide.

Writing in Response to Informational Text

Sometimes we read written material to learn something more about a subject or to learn something new. There are times when we are expected to analyze and reflect on what we read.

In this lesson, we shall practice active reading as we examine a nonfiction (informational) account from John Adams.

"Mr. Jefferson came into Congress, in June, 1775, and brought with him a reputation for literature, science, and a happy talent of composition. Writings of his were handed about, remarkable for the peculiar felicity of expression. Though a silent member in Congress, he was so prompt, frank, explicit, and decisive upon committees and in conversation—not even Samuel Adams was more so—that he soon seized upon my heart; and upon this occasion I gave him my vote, and did all in my power to procure the votes of others. I think he had one more vote than any other, and that placed him at the head of the committee. I had the next highest number, and that placed me second. The committee met, discussed the subject, and then appointed Mr. Jefferson and me to make the draft, I suppose because we were the two first on the list.

The subcommittee met. Jefferson proposed to me to make the draft. I said, 'I will not,' 'You should do it.'

'Oh! no.'

'Why will you not? You ought to do it.'

'I will not.'

'Why?'

'Reasons enough.'

'What can be your reasons?'

'Reason first, you are a Virginian, and a Virginian ought to appear at the head of this business. Reason second, I am obnoxious, suspected, and unpopular. You are very much otherwise. Reason third, you can write ten times better than I can.'

'Well,' said Jefferson, 'if you are decided, I will do as well as I can.'

'Very well. When you have drawn it up, we will have a meeting.'"

Practice   After carefully reading the excerpt, answer the following questions. You may work by yourself, with your teacher, or with other students. Remember to use present tense as you write.

1. Who wrote this excerpt? Why do you know that he is not "obnoxious, suspected, and unpopular"?

2. What is author's opinion of Thomas Jefferson?

3. Does Thomas Jefferson respect John Adams? How does the reader know?

4. How does the reader know that both Thomas Jefferson and John Adams are respected by others?

5. How does the reader know that Thomas Jefferson is a willing and humble leader?

When your answers to these questions are complete, compare them to those in the Teacher Guide.

More Practice Lesson 2

Circle the simple subject and underline the simple predicate in each sentence.

1. Ice melts.

2. Water changes from solid to liquid.

3. Water evaporates.

4. Water becomes vapor, a gas.

5. The water molecules remain the same.

6. Scientists write H_2O.

7. Our bodies need water.

8. Did you drink your water?

9. We need eight glasses daily.

10. Is the well dry?

11. We must conserve water.

12. Have you seen Niagara Falls?

13. Water is heavy.

14. A pint weighs about a pound.

15. A gallon weighs about eight pounds.

16. Can you swim?

17. The water holds you up.

18. Our bodies can float.

19. Swimming strengthens our muscles.

20. Mr. Pemberton swam the English Channel.

Write a capital letter on each letter that should be capitalized in these sentences.

1. the highest elevation in the united states is mount mckinley, alaska, at 20,320 feet.

2. the lowest elevation in the united states is in death valley, california, at 282 feet below sea level.

3. the deepest lake in the u.s. is crater lake in oregon.

4. the highest waterfall in north america is yosemite falls in yosemite, california.

5. have you ever seen the empire state building in new york city?

6. i read the poem "the road not taken" by robert frost.

7. robert attends charles e. gidley school in el monte, california.

8. mrs. rivas teaches at mercer college in new jersey.

9. the united states is half the size of russia and slightly smaller than china.

10. the mississippi river flows into the gulf of mexico.

11. have you ever swum in the pacific ocean?

12. peggy and ed dive deep in the atlantic ocean.

13. a building called the sears tower stands 1454 feet tall in chicago, illinois.

14. our largest national park, wrangell-st. elias, is located in alaska.

15. the appalachian mountains have lush green forests.

16. the curtises stayed in a town called big bear on saturday night.

17. next tuesday, february 20, mr. grouch will fly to a city in iowa called des moines.

18. have you seen the famous golden gate bridge in san francisco, california?

More Practice Lesson 9

Underline the entire verb phrase in each sentence.

1. By 1929, the Great Depression had come to the United States.

2. It had spread to Europe as well.

3. Many German workers had lost their jobs.

4. Germans were looking for a strong leader.

5. Hitler was making himself the absolute dictator.

6. Germans should have looked elsewhere for a leader.

7. Hitler was blaming Germany's problems on the Jews.

8. His systematic hatred and persecution of the Jews would lead to one of the most horrendous periods of history.

9. In 1938, Hitler was marching to conquer the world.

10. By April 1940, the Germans had conquered Denmark and Norway.

11. Hitler could have dominated all of Europe.

12. However, the British would not surrender.

13. Most Americans were sympathizing with Britain's lonely fight.

14. Should America have stayed out of the war?

15. President Franklin D. Roosevelt was saying this:

16. "America must become the arsenal of democracy."

17. Americans might have remained isolationists.

18. Meanwhile, the Japanese had been invading China.

19. The Japanese had formed an alliance with Germany.

20. On December 7, 1941, American soldiers at Pearl Harbor could see the red circles on the Japanese planes.

21. Your grandfather or great grandfather might have fought in World War II.

22. We shall remember the brave veterans, and we shall honor them always.

Silly Story #1
(After Lesson 10)

Harvest Stew

Teacher Instructions: Have the student number a blank, lined piece of paper from 1 to 24. Ask him or her to write an example of the indicated part of speech beside each number. Proceed slowly, and frequently question the student to be sure he or she has correct example of the part of speech you have requested for each blank space in the story. After the list has been completed, give the student a copy of "Harvest Stew." Ask him or her to write each word from the list in the blank space with the corresponding number. Then ask the student to read the story aloud.

Two friends, (1) _____ and (2)_____ ,
           proper noun (person)   proper noun (person)

who live in (3)_____ , made a harvest stew for their
              proper noun (place)

(4) _____ . First they placed some (5)_____
        feminine noun   concrete plural noun

and (6)_____ in the pot. They added a dash of
       concrete plural noun

(7) _____ and water, and they turned on the heat to
    concrete singular noun
    —neuter gender

(8) _____ degrees Fahrenheit. Delighted and excited,
        number

they (9) _____ and (10) _____ . They said,
        past tense action verb   past tense action verb

"We are a (11)_____ !"
              collective noun

When the stew began to boil, they tossed in a

(12) _____ and a (13) _____ for flavor.
     concrete singular noun   concrete, singular
                                   compound noun

They asked their friend, (14)_____, to taste it. Then
                             proper noun (person)

they chopped up some (15) _____ and diced a
                          concrete plural noun

(16) _____ for good measure.
     concrete singular noun

A (17) _____ watched them from the window.
          masculine noun

When he smelled the aroma, he began to (18) _____ .
                                              present tense
                                              action verb

The cooks ignored him and added (19) _____ more
                                          number

(20) _____ to the pot for color.
     concrete plural noun

The stew tasted so delicious, the cooks shared it with all

the (21)_____ in the neighborhood. Afterward, they
        plural noun
        —indefinite gender

felt full of (22) _____ and (23) _____ .
                 abstract singular noun   abstract singular noun

They happily gave the leftovers to (24) _____ .
                                        proper noun (person)

More Practice Lesson 20

Write a capital letter over each letter that should be capitalized in these sentences.

1. winston churchill declared, "we shall defend our island home . . . ."

2. have you read <u>the magic bicycle</u> by john bibee?

3. he also wrote <u>the only game in town</u>.

4. david and karen mains wrote <u>tales of the kingdom</u>.

5. they also wrote <u>tales of the resistance</u>.

6. I. stones
   A. where they are found
   B. what they contain

7. II. crystals
   A. how they are formed
   B. the story of granite

8. grandma reminded us, "a pint is a pound the world around."

9. oscar missed the school bus and forgot his tuesday homework, but at the end of the day he sighed, "all's well that ends well."

10. ruth and david elliott wrote <u>the richest kid in the poor house</u>.

11. president dwight d. eisenhower said, "the clearest way to show what the rule of law means to us in everyday life is to recall what has happened when there is no rule of law."

12. "why did the roman empire fall?" asked miss casey.

13. in 1776, thomas paine said, "what we obtain too cheap, we esteem too lightly."

14. "the germans should conquer and rule the world," hitler told his people.

15. anne frank wrote, "i can feel the suffering of millions . . . ."

16. edmund burke said, "the only thing necessary for the triumph of evil is for good men to do nothing."

Write a capital letter over each letter that should be capitalized in these sentences.

1. mr. and mrs. pérez teach spanish at portantorchas school in costa rica.

2. someday you might enjoy taking professor mhunzi's african american history class.

3. does grandpa speak french?

4. mrs. lópez excels in math and physics.

5. is your father learning to speak english?

6. i asked dad to have lunch with me.

7. when will rabbi feingold arrive?

8. did uncle bill play the trumpet last night?

9. i believe dr. yu is delivering a baby right now.

10. have you spoken with sergeant palusso or captain rice?

11. i helped mom clean the house and wash the cars.

12. have you helped your mother lately?

13. have you seen grandma moses's paintings?

14. my grandfather and i served meals to the homeless at bethany church in little rock, arkansas.

15. do aunt margaret and uncle charles play the french horn?

16. mrs. cordasco cooks delicious italian food.

17. did father spend the winter in bismarck, north dakota?

18. justin and trevor fixed mexican food for their brother jared.

19. james is studying biology, music, and russian history.

20. vice president ishigaki was always punctual.

Silly Story #2

(After Lesson 27)

Holiday Decor

(1)_____ and (2)_____ decided to
    proper noun (person)   proper noun (person)

decorate for the holiday party of the (3)_____.
                                            collective noun

"First of all," they agreed, "we (4)_____ and we
                                      future tense
                                      action verb

(5)_____ before we start." After (6)_____ and
    future tense   present participle
    action verb   form of a verb

(7)_____ for several hours, they had (8)_____
   present participle   past participle
   form of a verb   form of a verb

and (9)_____, and realized they had been
        past participle
        form of a verb

procrastinating. So they started to work without wasting any

more time.

They began decorating with (10)_____ lights
                                    descriptive adjective

and (11)_____ balloons (12)_____ the
        descriptive adjective   preposition

fireplace. They hung (13)_____ socks (14)_____
                        proper possessive   preposition
                        noun (person)

a (15)_____ for added (16)_____.
    concrete singular   abstract singular noun
    noun

When they had finished, there were (17)_____,
                                         descriptive adjective

(18)_____ decorations everywhere— (19)_____
  descriptive adjective   preposition

the tables, (20)_____ the walls, (21)_____ the
               preposition   preposition

doors, (22)_____ the windows, (23)_____
            preposition   preposition

the floors, and (24)_____ the ceilings. The decorators
                     preposition

(25)_____ (26)_____. It was a lovely sight.
    past tense   descriptive adjective
    linking verb
   (for a plural subject)

Underline each adjective in these sentences.

1. A channel is a deep, narrow body of water connecting two larger bodies of water.

2. The Polstein's son lives at the delta—a flat, sandy area at the mouth of the river.

3. Most people live on plains, which are flat, level areas of land.

4. Some people live in a canyon, a narrow valley with steep sides.

5. A harbor is a sheltered, safe place for ships to anchor.

6. This ship will enter that bay on its final voyage.

7. A sound is a wide channel linking two large bodies of water.

8. Many tourists enjoy beautiful Puget Sound in the Northwest.

9. The adventurous explorer wanted to climb the highest mountain in the world.

10. Europe's important waterway is the busy Rhine River.

11. The altitude of magnificent Mt. Everest is twenty-nine thousand twenty-eight feet.

12. Some mountain ranges form a boundary between two countries.

13. The mountainous continent of Asia has the most people.

14. Antarctica is a continent with no native human population.

15. The circumference of the earth is twenty-five thousand miles.

16. The earth's diameter is eight thousand miles.

17. The hot, humid rain forests in tropical regions have tall trees and heavy vines.

18. In hot, savanna regions, some trees and tall, tough grasses grow.

Underline every capital letter that does not belong in these sentences.

1. I saw a Rhinoceros, a Hippopotamus, and an African Elephant at the San Diego Zoo.

2. Mrs. Wellbaum grows Pecans and English Walnuts.

3. She has also planted Daisies, Geraniums, and African Violets.

4. Do you prefer German Chocolate Cake or Fudge Brownies?

5. The students played Soccer, Volleyball, and Tennis in gym class.

6. Gretchen was studying Math, Biology, and Geology when she caught the Chicken Pox.

7. I like Tacos, Burritos, and Enchiladas, but he prefers Chinese Food.

8. In the Spring, I will plant Italian Squash, Tomatoes, and Cucumbers.

9. We pick our Apricots, Peaches, and Plums in the Summer.

10. Next Fall, the Halls will return to the East Coast.

11. During the Winter, perhaps the Steinbrons will visit the West Coast.

12. Mr. Zee is recovering from a bad case of Tonsillitis.

13. Last Fall, he was tested for illnesses such as Malaria, Tuberculosis, and Hepatitis.

14. For entertainment, he plays Charades and does Crossword Puzzles.

15. He longs for his favorite foods: Fried Rice, Spaghetti, and Nachos with French Peas.

16. I bought some tasty Danish Pastries at a bakery in a Town called Solvang.

For 1–5, complete the partially constructed sentence diagram.

1. King Tut and Queen Hatshepsut lived in ancient Egypt.

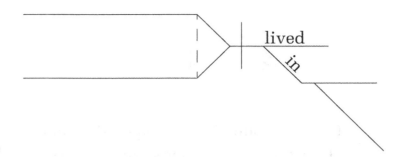

2. Treasure, weapons, and food filled Egyptian tombs.

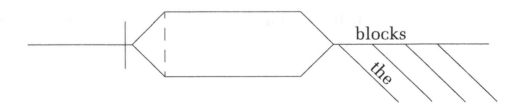

3. Egyptians hammered and dragged the huge, rough stone blocks.

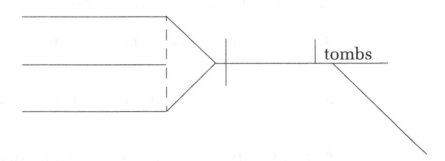

4. The Phoenicians sailed the Mediterranean, traded their goods, and developed an alphabet.

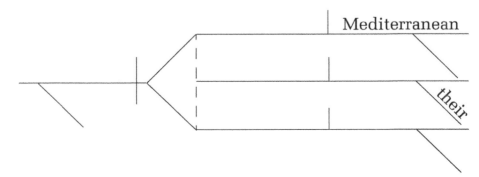

5. The Hittites conquered and oppressed other ancient kingdoms.

On a separate piece of paper, diagram sentences 6–13.

6. Mountains, deserts, and rivers divide the country of India.

7. People in ancient India counted, measured, and wrote.

8. Indian farmers and family groups plowed, planted, and harvested.

9. Hindu temples and shrines represent and honor the many Hindu gods.

10. Ancient Indians invented chess, polo, and playing cards.

11. The people rode camels, oxen, and elephants.

12. Cattle and other animals received special treatment.

13. India's flag features a gold stripe and a green stripe.

For 1 and 2, add periods where they are needed in the following outlines.

1. I Geography facts
   A Hemispheres
   B Continents
   C Oceans

2. II Land forms
   A Plains
   B Mountains
   C Plateaus

For 3–12, add periods where they are needed.

3. Richard M Nixon became president in 1969

4. Lyndon B Johnson became president after John F Kennedy was assassinated in 1963

5. Choose your friends carefully

6. Think before you speak

7. She dated her letter Sun, Nov 4, 2001

8. My phone bill was over $9500 (ninety-five dollars) last month!

9. Gen Robert E Lee said to his son, "Never do a wrong thing to make a friend or keep one"

10. Mail this package to:

    Ms Petunia U Blossom
    5722 W Magnolia Rd
    Bloomsville, Utah 84490

11. She likes baseball, basketball, football, etc, but she doesn't like hockey

12. Scot rarely goes to bed before 11 pm

For 13–15, write the months of the year whose names we do not abbreviate.

13. _____ 14. _____ 15. _____

For 16–19, use decimal points and numerals to write these numbers in the blanks.

16. _____ twenty dollars and forty-three cents

17. _____ sixteen and fifty-two hundredths

18. _____ ten and thirteen hundredths

19. _____ three dollars and fifty cents

Place commas wherever they are needed in these sentences.

1. On June 28 1914 a Serbian assassinated the heir to the Austrian throne.

2. World War I began on July 28 1914 when Austria declared war on Serbia.

3. Russia mobilized for conflict on July 30 1914.

4. On August 1 1914 Germany declared war on Russia.

5. Germany declared war on France on August 3.

6. Germany Austria-Hungary and Italy made up the Triple Alliance.

7. The Triple Entente included Great Britain France and Russia.

8. On April 6 1917 Congress declared war on Germany.

9. Private organizations like the Red Cross the YMCA the Salvation Army the Knights of Columbus and the Jewish Welfare Board helped in the war effort.

10. On November 11 1918 in Compiègne France representatives of the Allies as well as those of Germany signed an armistice to end the war.

11. The Peace Conference convened January 18 1919 at a palace called Versailles.

12. Versailles is located outside of Paris France.

13. President Woodrow Wilson collapsed after delivering a speech in Pueblo Colorado on September 25 1919.

For 14–17, place commas where they are needed in these addresses.

14. 11147 Bunbury Street Saint Louis Missouri

15. 270 Alta Vista Drive Tallahassee Florida

16. 4921 Cedar Avenue Topeka Kansas

17. 30 Pine Street Steamboat Springs Colorado

Silly Story #3

(After Lesson 48)

A Love Story   (1) _____ could hardly wait until Valentine's
                         proper noun (feminine)

Day. She loved Brock Lee and planned a (2) _____
                                            descriptive adjective

surprise for him. She thought, "Brock Lee is (3) _____
                                                  comparative adjective

and (4) _____than any other man I know. In fact, he
         comparative adjective

is the (5) _____ man in the whole world."
            superlative adjective

To be nice, she would first (6) _____ and
                                 present tense transitive verb

(7) _____ him. Perhaps she would give him an
     present tense transitive verb

unusual (8) _____ (9) _____ to prove her
             descriptive adjective   concrete singular noun

(10) _____ for him.
      abstract singular noun

She began searching for the perfect gift. She looked

(11) _____ stores, (12) _____ malls, (13) _____
      preposition   preposition   preposition

catalogs, and under every single (14) _____ and
                                        concrete singular noun

(15) _____. Finally, she decided to give him a
      concrete singular noun

(16) _____ and two (17) _____.
      concrete singular noun   concrete plural noun

After wrapping this (18) _____ of presents, she
                          superlative adjective

called Brock Lee on the telephone. When he said hello, she

(19) _____ (20) _____ (21) _____.
      past tense action verb   coordinating   past tense action verb
         (intransitive)   conjunction   (intransitive)

She could hardly speak.

Finally, she stammered, "Brock, I would like to invite you

to (22) _proper noun (place)_ for dinner. I have a (23) descriptive adjective present for you. You are the (24) _____ in the

superlative adjective

world. You are (25) _____than my father. I love

comparative adjective

you more than (26) _____ or (27) _____.

concrete plural noun   concrete plural noun

All I have to do is think about you and my heart is full of

(28) _____."

abstract singular noun

There was a long, (29) _____ pause. Then a

descriptive adjective

strange man said in a (30) _____ voice, "I'm sorry,

descriptive adjective

but you must have the wrong number."

Place commas where they are needed in these sentences.

1. Joshua where are you going?

2. Christina I need your help!

3. Are you ready for spaghetti Freddy?

4. Why Margarita did you bring your dog to school?

5. American businessman Henry Ford brought the country its first affordable car the Model T.

6. The Model T came in one color black.

7. My next door neighbor a collector of antique cars is restoring a Model T in his garage.

8. He won't paint it green my favorite color even though his wife Betty and I think it would look snazzy.

9. Emily Ishigaki President shared some interesting facts with the school board.

10. Mr. Seymour the Superintendent encouraged the teachers.

11. I believe Miss Ngo Class Treasurer should collect the money.

12. The authors included Herbert Zamora Ph.D. and Mauricio Zelaya D.D.S.

13. Patricia Childress R.N. works at City of Hope in Duarte California.

14. Yuan Chen D.D.S. pulled my tooth.

15. Gloria Quigley M.D. prescribed the antibiotics.

16. I see that Freddy Rivas M.Div. is your new pastor.

17. Our superintendent James Dawson Ed.D. is quite a guy.

18. Allison are you trying to be punctual?

19. Did you call me last night Henry?

20. I think dear cousin that you need a plumber.

Place commas where they are needed in 1–12.

1. Dear Kerry

Please feed Snooper.

Love
Mom

2. Hi Mom

I fed Snooper.

Love
Kerry

3. Hey Joe

Please wait for me after school today.

Your friend
Moe

4. The index listed "Webster Noah" on page 320.

5. Under the *p*'s, I found the name "Pizarro Francisco."

6. According to the index, "Revere Paul" can be found on page 227.

7. I wrote "Hake Danielle" because it asked for last name first.

8. My friend wrote "Placencia Betty."

9. Dear Grandpa

My email address has changed to pedro@quickmail.com.

Your grandson
Pedro

10. Dear Pedro

Thanks for sending me your new address. I hope you're enjoying school.

Love
Grandpa

11. Dear Friends

Thank you for the surprise party!

Gratefully
Bernardo

12. Dear Mrs. Villalobos

I'm sorry you are sick. My prayers are with you.

Sincerely
Docker Busick

More Practice Lesson 56

Place commas where they are needed in these sentences.

1. Abraham Lincoln we remember did not let his childhood poverty and hardships deprive him of a successful life.

2. Through diligence and integrity we recall he became a respected lawyer and statesman.

3. No he never allowed the bitterness of the Civil War to make him a bitter man.

4. Yes he was determined to stand for what he believed was right.

5. Lincoln I have heard was known for his wit and his funny stories.

6. His sense of humor I think saw him through the dark trials of a long Civil War.

7. Lincoln never lost contact with the common people even after he became famous.

8. Despite his busy schedule he always found time to listen to all who came to seek his aid.

9. With unyielding persistence Lincoln guided the nation through crisis.

10. No President with the possible exception of George Washington is held dearer in the hearts of the American people.

11. Abraham Lincoln illustrates better than perhaps any other hero the qualities that have made America great.

12. Certainly his integrity and kindness toward all people represent American values.

13. In addition his courage and determination display the American tradition.

14. Therefore we hold the memory of Abraham Lincoln in high esteem.

15. He is without doubt a true hero.

Underline the dependent clause in each sentence, and star the subordinating conjunction.

1. Although George Washington Carver was born into slavery, he became one of the world's greatest contributors to agriculture.

2. I have heard that he also sang and played the organ.

3. When he was very young, George was keenly interested in plants.

4. While he was still a boy, people nicknamed him "the plant doctor."

5. After he graduated from high school, he enrolled at Simpson College in Iowa.

6. He cooked, took in laundry, and worked as a janitor so that he could pay his college expenses.

7. In the 1890's, Iowa State Agricultural College honored him because he had collected 20,000 species of fungi.

8. Even though he had a promising career at Iowa State, he gave it up to help black students in the South.

9. He joined the Tuskegee Institute because he wanted to improve southern agriculture.

10. Wherever he went, he taught how to improve farming methods and conserve natural resources.

11. Whenever someone needed him, he was there.

12. While cotton was the major crop of the South, it seriously depleted the soil.

13. Peanuts would help nourish the soil if they became a profitable crop.

14. He hoped that he could think of more ways to use peanuts.

15. After Carver discovered three hundred uses for the peanut, farmers began planting more peanuts.

16. Peanuts became more and more popular until they were one of the most important cash crops in the South.

17. Though Professor Carver became world famous for his research, he led a modest and quiet life.

18. While Carver had achieved unquestioned greatness, he remained a humble servant throughout his life.

19. I understand that he also taught Sunday school.

20. People recognized that his chief desire was to serve humanity.

Place commas where they are needed in these sentences.

1. Are you aware that half the states in the U.S. have Native American names?

2. Hiawatha was a peace-loving influential Mohawk chief who wanted to end tribal wars.

3. Pilgrims and Native Americans worked together to survive the long cold cruel New England winters.

4. Because he taught the Pilgrims many things about wilderness living Samoset became a friend of the Pilgrims.

5. I understand that he introduced the Pilgrims to Massasoit Chief of the Wampanoag people.

6. After they signed a treaty with the Pilgrims the Wampanoag shared the first Thanksgiving with them.

7. Tecumseh was a clever courageous Shawnee chief.

8. As soon as he had united other tribes he led them against the U.S. in the War of 1812.

9. Since Sequoyah had a genius for language he devised a written alphabet of 86 characters for the Cherokees.

10. Because they had an alphabet the Cherokees published their own books and newspapers.

11. The beautiful forested Sequoia National Park and the magnificent Sequoia tree are named after this famous ingenious Native American.

12. Sacajawea was a strong adventurous Shoshone woman who guided the Lewis and Clark expedition across the West.

13. Before General Custer knew what was happening Sitting Bull was attacking his army.

14. If Crazy Horse had not fought in the battle the Sioux might not have won the war.

15. Black Hawk didn't know that his great-grandson would be Jim Thorpe one of the greatest athletes in history.

Place commas where they are needed in these sentences.

1. General Robert E. Lee told his son "Do not appear to others what you are not."

2. He also said "Deal kindly but firmly with all your classmates."

3. Will Rogers said "I never met a man I didn't like."

4. "Labor to keep alive... that little spark of celestial fire called conscience" said George Washington.

5. "If you stand for nothing you'll fall for anything" Mom always said.

6. Confucius said "Virtue is not left to stand alone."

7. He continued "He who practices it will have neighbors."

8. Virtue is goodness and its opposite is vice.

9. Greed is a vice but self-discipline is a virtue.

10. Be kind to animals for they depend on us.

11. We can have virtues or we can have vices.

12. The woman was poor yet she gave her last few cents.

13. He did not lie nor did he cheat.

14. He told the truth for he had integrity.

15. If you are always honest people will trust you.

16. Friends will respect you if you admit a mistake.

17. Dad says that we should be considerate of others.

18. We can try to be virtuous but we will never be perfect.

19. David said "Becky there are lots of ways to help out."

20. Becky was free that day so she cheerfully volunteered.

More Practice Lesson 69

Place quotation marks where they are needed in these sentences.

1. Benjamin Franklin said, A good conscience is a continual Christmas.

2. I cannot live without books, said Thomas Jefferson to John Adams.

3. Some books are to be tasted, said Francis Bacon, others to be swallowed, and some few to be chewed and digested.

4. The following words were written by British author Samuel Butler: Books are like imprisoned souls till someone takes them down from a shelf and frees them.

5. Theodore Roosevelt said, Books are almost as individual as friends.

6. Friendship, said Thomas Fuller, is not to be bought.

7. Friendships multiply joys and divide griefs, said H. G. Bohn.

8. Edward Young said, Procrastination is the thief of time.

9. Never put off till tomorrow what you can do today, Lord Chesterfield told his son.

10. Aunt Delanah reminded us about the importance of good study skills.

11. Hesiod lived in Greece approximately 2800 years ago. Diligence increaseth the fruit of toil, he wrote in the eighth century B.C.

12. Life is a long lesson in humility, wrote James Barrie in 1891.

13. Sharia's mother asked her to be a good example for her little sister.

14. It is hard to be high and humble, wrote Thomas Fuller in 1732.

15. I worked hard for that *A*, said Johnna.

For 1–16, place quotation marks where they are needed in the following dialogues.

From *Little Women* by Louisa May Alcott:

1. Army shoes, best to be had, cried Jo.

2. Some handkerchiefs, all hemmed, said Beth.

3. I'll get a little bottle of cologne. She likes it, and it won't cost much, so I'll have some left to buy my pencils, added Amy.

4. How will we give the things? asked Meg.

From *The Swiss Family Robinson* by Johann Wyss:

5. What? Ho! are they really coconuts? cried Ernest. Do let me take them again, Mother, do let me look at them.

6. No, thank you, replied my wife, with a smile. I have no wish to see you again overburdened.

7. Oh, but I have only to throw away these sticks, which are of no use, and then I can easily carry them.

8. Worse and worse, said Fritz. I have a particular regard for those heavy, useless sticks. Did you ever hear of sugar cane?

From *The Adventures of Tom Sawyer* by Mark Twain:

9. What is it! exclaimed Joe, under his breath.

10. I wonder, said Tom in a whisper.

11. 'Tain't thunder, said Huckleberry, in an awed tone, because thunder—

12. Hark! said Tom. Listen—don't talk.

From *Alice in Wonderland* by Lewis Carroll:

13. Living backwards! Alice repeated in great astonishment. I never heard of such a thing.

14. —but there's one great advantage in it, that one's memory works both ways.

15. I'm sure *mine* only works one way, Alice remarked. I can't remember things before they happen.

16. It's a poor sort of memory that only works backwards, the Queen remarked.

(continued)

For 17–30, enclose titles of short literary works and songs in quotation marks.

17. Oliver Wendell Holmes wrote a poem called The Chambered Nautilus.

18. Charles Finney, an early American revivalist, preached a sermon entitled Selfishness.

19. Josh Billings (1818-1885) wrote a humorous essay called The Bumblebee.

20. We read Nathaniel Hawthorne's short story The Great Carbuncle.

21. This interesting article, called How to Clean Your Windows, came from Sunday's newspaper.

22. Marco wrote an editorial for the newspaper and titled it Experimental Educational Reform.

23. A Listening Heart is the name of Jayne's poem about friendship.

24. Dog Heroes is the name of the magazine article that sparked my interest.

25. For his history class, John wrote an essay called The Hydrogen Bomb.

26. For his English class, James wrote a fictional story and titled it The Grandfather Clock.

27. Professor Gallop gave a lecture entitled Who's Afraid of the Big Square Root?

28. Jeannie with the Light Brown Hair was written by Stephen Foster in 1854.

29. Francis Bacon (1561-1626), an English philosopher, scientist, and writer, wrote an essay called On Revenge.

30. Shakespeare's poem When Icicles Hang by the Wall was a favorite in Mrs. McPhail's class.

Silly Story #4
(After Lesson 72)

Planting a Garden

Spring always gave (1) _____ the urge to plant a
<u>proper noun</u>
<u>(person; masculine)</u>

garden. This year, (2) _____ and (3) _____
<u>abstract noun</u>   <u>abstract noun</u>

filled his head along with thoughts of having the

(4) _____ garden of all the neighbors in
<u>superlative adjective</u>

(5) _____ . "My (6) _____ garden will be
<u>noun (place)</u>   <u>descriptive adjective</u>

(7) _____ than (8) _____ , (9) _____ , or
<u>comparative adjective</u>   <u>possessive pronoun</u>   <u>possessive pronoun</u>

(10) _____ ," he thought.
<u>possessive pronoun</u>

In preparation, he (11) _____ the soil while
<u>past tense transitive verb</u>

eyeing the neighbors. He wondered if (12) _____
<u>proper noun</u>
<u>(person; feminine)</u>

and (13) _____ were spying on him. He would
<u>proper noun</u>
<u>(person; masculine)</u>

outdo (14) _____ and (15) _____ .
<u>nominative case</u>   <u>nominative case</u>
<u>personal pronoun (feminine)</u> <u>personal pronoun (masculine)</u>

After (16) _____ and (17) _____ for
<u>present participle</u>   <u>present participle</u>
<u>form of verb</u>   <u>form of verb</u>

several hours, he began planting. First, he planted two

(18) _____ . He hummed as he planted a row of
<u>concrete noun, plural</u>

(19) _____ (20) _____ . In a very deep hole,
<u>adjective (number)</u>   <u>concrete noun, plural</u>

he placed a (21) _____ and surrounded it with
<u>concrete noun, singular</u>

(22) _____ marigolds. Next, he covered the entire
<u>descriptive adjective</u>

garden with his (23) _____ mixture of fertilizer
<u>superlative adjective</u>

made from old (24) _____ and (25) _____ .
<u>concrete noun, plural</u>   <u>concrete noun, plural</u>

Finally, he sat down and waited for his garden to grow,

satisfied that no one else would have (26) _____
<u>comparative adjective</u>

results than he.

Underline all words that should be italicized in print.

1. Mom's favorite movie is The Sound of Music.

2. Uncle Charles reads The New York Times newspaper every morning.

3. Have you seen the musical drama called Annie?

4. Caleb listens to a music CD entitled The Lost Boys.

5. Have you read the novel Moby Dick by Herman Melville?

6. While in the Navy, Rick served on the aircraft carrier U.S.S. Constitution.

7. David named his airplane the Pelican II.

8. If you visit the Louvre in Paris, you might see Rembrandt's painting called Bathsheba.

9. Rembrandt also painted The Jewish Bride, which you can see in a museum in Amsterdam.

10. My brother doesn't like opera, but we went to see The Magic Flute anyway.

11. Please use the word dilemma in a sentence.

12. In 1915, the Germans attacked a large British luxury ship, the Lusitania, and sank it.

13. Its scientific name is corvus brachyrhynchos, but we usually call it a crow.

14. In 1848, Karl Marx published a book called The Communist Manifesto.

15. We learned today what the German word gemütlichkeit means.

16. Columbus sailed to the new world in a ship called the Santa Maria.

Complete this irregular verb chart by writing the past and past participle forms of each verb.

VERB	PAST	PAST PARTICIPLE
1. beat	_____	_____
2. bite	_____	_____
3. bring	_____	_____
4. build	_____	_____
5. burst	_____	_____
6. buy	_____	_____
7. catch	_____	_____
8. come	_____	_____
9. cost	_____	_____
10. dive	_____	_____
11. drag	_____	_____
12. draw	_____	_____
13. drown	_____	_____
14. drive	_____	_____
15. eat	_____	_____
16. fall	_____	_____
17. feel	_____	_____
18. fight	_____	_____
19. find	_____	_____
20. flee	_____	_____
21. fly	_____	_____
22. forget	_____	_____
23. forgive	_____	_____

**More Practice
Lesson 74
(Continued)**

Write the correct verb form for each sentence.

1. Yesterday the Blues (beated, beat) the Reds in ping pong.

2. The Blues have (beat, beaten) them in every tournament.

3. For yesterday's picnic, I (brang, brought) sandwiches.

4. I have always (brung, brought) sandwiches.

5. Last year they (builded, built) a new house.

6. They have (builded, built) two houses.

7. Tom (buyed, bought) Christina a ring.

8. He has (buyed, bought) a beautiful one.

9. Steve (catched, caught) a cold.

10. I think he has (catched, caught) a nasty one.

11. John (comed, came) home early.

12. He has (came, come) home to rest.

13. Yesterday bananas (costed, cost) 49¢ a pound.

14. They have (cost, costed) more in the past.

15. Miss Muffett (dove, dived) into the lake.

16. She has (dove, dived) often.

17. Kurt (drawed, drew) a picture.

18. He has (drawed, drawn) several.

19. Daniel (drived, drove) around the block.

20. He has (drove, driven) for ten years.

21. A branch (falled, fell) out of the tree.

22. Branches have (falled, fell, fallen) every year.

23. Two cats (fighted, fought) last night.

24. They have (fighted, fought) every night this week.

25. A bird (flied, flew) by.

26. The bird has (flew, flown) to its nest.

Complete this irregular verb chart by writing the past and past participle forms of each verb.

VERB	PAST	PAST PARTICIPLE
1. get	_____	_____
2. give	_____	_____
3. go	_____	_____
4. hang (execute)	_____	_____
5. hang (suspend)	_____	_____
6. hide	_____	_____
7. hold	_____	_____
8. keep	_____	_____
9. lay (place)	_____	_____
10. lead	_____	_____
11. lend	_____	_____
12. lie (recline)	_____	_____
13. lie (deceive)	_____	_____
14. lose	_____	_____
15. make	_____	_____
16. mistake	_____	_____
17. put	_____	_____
18. ride	_____	_____
19. rise	_____	_____
20. run	_____	_____
21. see	_____	_____
22. sell	_____	_____

Choose the correct verb form for each sentence.

1. Bob (gived, gave) a report to the committee.

2. He has (gived, gave, given) a report each month.

3. Joshua (goed, went) to a new country.

4. He has (went, gone) alone.

5. I (hanged, hung) a picture on the wall.

6. I have (hanged, hung) three pictures.

7. The pirate (hided, hid) the treasure.

8. He (holded, held) a gold coin.

9. He has (keeped, kept) the coin for years.

10. Jan (layed, laid) the book on the table.

11. She has (layed, laid) several books on the table.

12. He was tired, so he (laid, lay) on the bed.

13. He has (laid, lain) there for hours!

14. Christie (losed, lost) her keys again.

15. She has (losed, lost) them twice already today.

16. I (maked, made) a mistake.

17. I have (maked, made) many mistakes.

18. Yesterday, I (putted, put) toothpaste on my hairbrush.

19. I have never before (putted, put) toothpaste on anything but a toothbrush.

20. The sun (rised, rose) at 6 a.m.

21. It has (risen, rosen) earlier each morning.

22. I (seen, saw) you earlier.

23. I have (seen, saw) you every day.

24. He (selled, sold) his bike.

25. He has (selled, sold) two bikes.

Complete this irregular verb chart by writing the past and past participle forms of each verb.

VERB	PAST	PAST PARTICIPLE
1. set		
2. shake		
3. shine (light)		
4. shine (polish)		
5. shut		
6. sit		
7. slay		
8. sleep		
9. spring		
10. stand		
11. strive		
12. swim		
13. swing		
14. take		
15. teach		
16. tell		
17. think		
18. wake		
19. weave		
20. wring		
21. write		

Choose the correct verb form for each sentence.

1. Jen (setted, set) the table.

2. She has (setted, set) it for each meal.

3. She (shook, shaked) his hand.

4. She has (shaked, shaken) many hands.

5. A light (shined, shone) in the darkness.

6. The light has (shined, shone) each night.

7. Rich (shined, shone) his shoes.

8. He has (shined, shone) several pairs of shoes today.

9. Isabel (shutted, shut) the library door.

10. She has (shutted, shut) the door every evening.

11. She (sitted, sat) on a rock.

12. She has (sitted, sat) there for hours.

13. I (slept, sleeped) twelve hours last night.

14. I have never (slept, sleeped) so long.

15. He (standed, stood) on his feet.

16. He has (standed, stood) there all day.

17. I (swam, swum) a mile this morning.

18. I have (swam, swum) three miles this week.

19. He (taked, took) his dog to the vet.

20. He has (took, taken) Spot to the vet twice this month.

21. Alba and Blanca (teached, taught) me to speak Spanish.

22. They have (teached, taught) me many new words.

23. Ilbea (telled, told) me a secret.

24. Has she (telled, told) you the news?

25. I (thinked, thought) you were wise.

26. I have always (thinked, thought) that.

Underline each adverb in these sentences.

1. Today, I was somewhat surprised when a peacock strutted proudly into my yard.

2. When he carelessly stepped on our flowers, I was rather annoyed.

3. I was completely amazed at the dazzling colors in his tail feathers.

4. I had never seen anything like it before.

5. I quickly grabbed my camera to photograph this lovely sight.

6. Then, with a thump, a peahen landed clumsily on my roof.

7. I'm not quite sure why they came here.

8. The peacock hungrily gobbled the petunias that we had so carefully planted.

9. The peahen eagerly uprooted some daffodils and gingerly nibbled the ferns that waved too close to her beak.

10. Screeching loudly, the two birds soon flew away.

11. I really hope Mom won't be too upset when she sees the extremely messy condition of the garden.

12. I'm so glad the peafowl visited here!

13. I hope they come back tomorrow.

14. I could simply invite them inside.

15. If they'd sit down politely, I would happily offer them some broccoli and carrots.

16. I can almost see them now.

17. Would they gracefully accept my hospitality?

18. Would Mom ever forgive me?

Replace commas with semicolons where they are needed in these sentences.

1. Cities with Native American names include Wichita, Kansas, Tucson, Arizona, Tallahassee, Florida, Minneapolis, Minnesota, and Seminole, Oklahoma.

2. The sales representative passes through Denver, Colorado, Austin, Texas, and Memphis, Tennessee.

3. Damien plays drums, Annie plays the saxophone, the flute, and the trumpet.

4. Broccoli, okra, and asparagus are vegetables, tangerines, apricots, and nectarines are fruits.

5. Dr. Hagelganz spoke this week, moreover, Foster Shannon will speak next week.

6. James washed the car, cleaned the house, and mowed the lawn, consequently, he fell asleep during the movie.

7. I like to bake cookies, cakes, and pies, however, I've never made an eclair.

8. In November a pound of bananas cost 29¢, in December, 39¢, in January, 49¢, in February, 59¢, and in March, 69¢.

9. I worked all day, therefore, I finished the project on time.

10. Donald and Tim will be there, also, Cecilia will come if she can.

11. She enjoys planting trees, for example, she planted two oaks and a cedar last fall.

12. Joe cleaned the kitchen, furthermore, he organized all the cupboards and drawers.

13. The weather was cold, nevertheless, Bob hiked to the top of the mountain.

14. He wore new shoes, as a result, he has blisters on his feet.

15. Would you rather visit Paris, France, Rome, Italy, Juneau, Alaska, or Moscow, Russia?

Silly Story #5
(After Lesson 93)

Packing a Suitcase

Three friends, (1) _____, (2) _____,
proper noun, person proper noun, person

and (3) _____, were planning a long trip to
proper noun, person

(4) _____. (5) _____, they began
proper noun, place adverb that tells "how"

thinking about what they should pack for this

(6) _____ journey.
descriptive adjective

First, they found the (7) _____ suitcases. Then
superlative adjective

they looked (8) _____ and (9) _____
adverb that tells "where" adverb that tells "where"

for some stylish (10) _____ clothes.
descriptive adjective

(11) _____ they (12) _____ as they
adverb that tells "when" past tense action verb

packed (13) _____ and (14) _____ in
concrete plural noun concrete plural noun

case of bad weather.

Full of anticipation and (15) _____, the
abstract noun

friends (16) _____ loaded their suitcases with
adverb that tells "how"

(17) _____ (18) _____. They wondered
number adjective concrete plural noun

if they should also bring some (19) _____.
concrete plural noun

They borrowed (20) _____ earplugs and
proper noun (person), possessive case

(21) _____ toothbrush for the trip, and they
proper noun (person), possessive case

(22) _____ purchased a (23) _____. As
adverb that tells "how" concrete singular noun

they packed, they discussed (24) _____ and
abstract noun

(25) _____ until late at night.
abstract noun

Unfortunately, the three friends were too exhausted to travel the next day. "Forget the trip," they said. "Let's

(26) _____ instead."

    action verb: *first person plural,*
    present tense, intransitive

Insert apostrophes where they are needed in these sentences.

1. He couldnt remember whether hed last seen the doctor back in 47 or 52.

2. Dont you want to remove the extra *xs* from this page?

3. In her letters, Grandma writes *xs* and *os* to indicate kisses and hugs.

4. Mrs. Jones yelled, "Good mornin!" to her neighbor.

5. "Oh my," exclaimed Sue, "Those ladies were just walkin and talkin, and they never saw the thief comin!"

6. Cant you see that I havent time to go out for lunch?

7. She graduated from high school with the class of 70, but I graduated in 66.

8. Isnt her integrity obvious?

9. Were going to class. Arent you?

10. Theyre going to class also.

11. Wouldnt you like to join us?

12. Shouldnt we try to be punctual?

13. Shell come if she can.

14. Well forgive her if she doesnt come.

15. Ive written him, but he hasnt responded.

16. Shed received nothing but *As* all year.

17. They couldnt see through the fog.

18. They werent sure where their cars were.

19. He doesnt know youre home.

20. She hasnt called yet, but shell call before noon.